QUAINT ESSENTIAL NEW ORLEANS

QUAINT ESSENTIAL NEW ORLEANS

A
Crescent City
Lexicon

Kevin J. Bozant

Po-Boy Press - New Orleans

QUAINT ESSENTIAL NEW ORLEANS

No portion of this book may be reproduced in any form,
analog or digital, without written permission from
Po-Boy Press.

Text & Photographs
Copyright © 2012 Kevin J. Bozant

poboypress@yahoo.com
www.amazon.com/author/kevinjbozant

All rights reserved

ISBN-13: 978-1469951102

Books available from
Po-Boy Press – New Orleans

African American New Orleans:
A Guide to 100 Civil Rights, Culture & Jazz Sites

ISBN-13: 978-1466410589

Quaint Essential New Orleans:
A Crescent City Lexicon

ISBN-13: 978-1469951102

Crescent City Soldiers:
Military Monuments of New Orleans

ISBN-13: 978-1449913915

Music Street New Orleans:
A Guide to 200 Jazz, Rock and Rhythm & Blues Sites

ISBN-13: 978-1484944998

Crescent City Saints:
Religious Icons of New Orleans

ISBN-13: 978-1494239695

www.amazon.com/author/kevinjbozant

Sample downloads available at:
www.independentauthornetwork.com/kevin-j-bozant.html

Do You Know What It Means To Mispronounce New Orleans?

NEW ORLEANS (new OR luns)
We never pronounce New Orleans (or LEENS) as you hear it in song. It is only sung that way because it rhymes with red beans and Creole queens. The common pronunciation is (new OR luns). The original French is Nouvelle Orleans (noo VELL or lee YAHN). Some of our Uptown neighbors will say (nyu OR lee uns), and we still agree to be seen with them. One notable exception is Irma Thomas - the Soul Queen of New (or LEENS)!

ACKNOWLEDGEMENTS

For the foreseeable future, the New Orleans narrative will be divided into two chapters: before and after Katrina. August 29th, 2005 represents a literal and figurative watershed to which our lives, culture, architecture and neighborhoods will be forever referenced. The physical loss of family and property remains etched into our hearts and souls. We also confronted the possibility that our cultural identity had washed away, leaving the spiritual damage irreparable.

Not so.

This book is the result of a life-long passion celebrating every nuance of New Orleans which has so thoroughly saturated my soul since the day I took my first steps along the banquettes of the Ninth Ward.

I would like to thank the following "quaint and essential" friends and relatives who took those same steps with me and contributed to this effort:

Norman & Pat Hellmers,
Michael and Lynne Riemer,
Alan Heintzen, Dennis Malloy, Woody Keim,
Diane Heintzen, Maryann Fikes
and my parents,
Joe and Helen Bozant

INTRODUCTION

If you write about New Orleans, get it right about New Orleans. In *Quaint Essential New Orleans,* Kevin J. Bozant takes you on an entertaining and personal journey through the Crescent City's culture of unique iconography, creative geography and mystifying terminology. He offers readers a generous serving from the colloquial melting pot with ingredients borrowed from the French, Spanish, Creoles, African Americans, Cajuns, West Indians, Irish, Italians, Germans, Native Americans, Canadians, Vietnamese and a smattering of Yat mixed in just to make your mom-n-em happy. The resulting mélange of creative and colorful references for streets, food, Mardi Gras, jazz, local characters, geography, history and culture, blends into a delicious gumbo of grammar which is often mispronounced, misinterpreted, misunderstood and misspelled.

Do you know the difference between, Mardi Gras and Carnival, Storyland and Storyville, roux and rue? Can you give directions to Dead Man's Curve, Monkey Wrench Corner or Pigeon Town? Can you name the Emperor of the World, the Voodoo Queen or the Chicken King? Do you know what it means to mispronounce New Orleans, banquette, Tchefuncte, flambeaux, Tchoupitoulas or lagniappe?

If you are producing a movie or documentary in New Orleans.
If you are writing or anchoring a local newscast.
If you are editing a city newspaper, magazine or website.
If you are writing a television series set in the Crescent City.
If your next novel is about New Orleans.
You Need This Book!

Quaint Essential New Orleans
190 pages – 675 entries – 200 photographs
Available on Amazon.com

If you visit your Mom-n-em for a crawfish boil, it's ok to "suck da heads," but remember, "don't eat the dead ones!"

ST. JOSEPH'S DAY ALTAR
St. Augustine Church - Tremé
March 2005

Quaint Essential New Orleans

A IS FOR ALLIGATOR PEAR

'AINTS is an unflattering nickname for the New Orleans Saints in the midst of a losing season. It is a term no longer in use. **See: Bag Heads, Benson Boogie, Bountygate, Who Dat?**

AIN'T DERE NO MORE is a lament made popular by Benny Grunch and the Bunch. The lyrics mourn the loss of the traditional landmarks that have vanished from the New Orleans landscape such as K&B, Schwegmann's, Krauss, Holmes, Pontchartrain Beach, Maison Blanche and many others. For a complete list, buy the CD. **See: Holmes, K&B Purple, Schwegmann's**

AIRLINE HIGHWAY/DRIVE Highway 61 runs from New Orleans to Baton Rouge and beyond. The stretch that runs through Jefferson Parish was changed to Airline Drive because it sounded more sophisticated. Really?
See: Earhart, Hammond Hwy.

AIRPLANE We love our boiled crabs heavy with meat and full of fat. If not, it's an "airplane" and we throw it out. In some neighborhoods you'll hear the term "kite."
See: Dead Men's Fingers, Loaded She

ALFÉREZ Enrique Alférez is one of Louisiana's most cherished sculptors. He created many artworks found in City Park and all around New Orleans. His name is often misspelled Alverez. **See: Popp Fountain**

ALGIERS POINT is a section of Orleans Parish located on the West Bank of the Mississippi River to the east of the French Quarter. Confused? The Point, once known as Slaughterhouse Point, is the historic part of Algiers and is connected to the CBD by ferry. The sharp right turn in the River is called Algiers Bend. **See: CBD, Kenner Bend, The Point, West Bank**

ALIX Street in Algiers Point can be found on some maps misspelled Alex. **See: Bouny Street**

ALLIGATOR Remember, we have alligators in Louisiana, not crocodiles! **See: Cocodrie**

ALLIGATOR PEAR is the traditional New Orleans term for an avocado. **See: Mirliton**

ALL SAINTS DAY is a special day in New Orleans when families gather at the city cemeteries to clean, repair and whitewash tombs. Antoinette K-Doe once hosted her annual picnic right in the middle of St. Louis Cemetery #2 near Ernie's K-Doe's tomb. **See: Cemeteries, Emperor of the World**

ALMONASTER (AL ma nast er) Historically, his name is spelled Don Andres Almonester y Roxas, but on the streets of New Orleans it is written in stone: Almonaster. The stretch of Almonaster that runs from Downman Road to Michoud is called the Almonaster Corridor. **See: Industrial Canal, Michoud**

AMITE (AY MEET), aka Amite City, is the parish seat of Tangipahoa Parish. Amite bills itself as the Oyster Capital of the World right smack in the heart of dairy country.
See: Parish, Tangipihoa

ANDOUILLE (ahn DOO wee) is a spicy smoked sausage made of pork, fat, salt, cracked black pepper and garlic; smoked over pecan wood and sugar cane. It is used in a variety of Louisiana dishes such as red beans and rice, jambalaya and gumbo. Not to be confused with andouillette sausage. LaPlace is the Andouille Capital of the World where a new Miss Andouille is chosen every year. Applications are being taken. **See: Gumbo, Jambalaya, LaPlace, Red Beans & Rice**

ANGOLA (an GO luh) is a town in West Feliciana Parish. It was the site of the Angola Plantation and is now a local synonym for prison. It is the location of the Louisiana State Penitentiary which hosts the annual Angola Prison Rodeo. Some R&B singers and former residents refer to it as the Ponderosa. **See: Feliciana, OPP**

ANTEBELLUM is a term used to describe the plantation houses along the banks of the Mississippi River. Ante means before and bellum means war, specifically, the Civil War. **See: Nottoway**

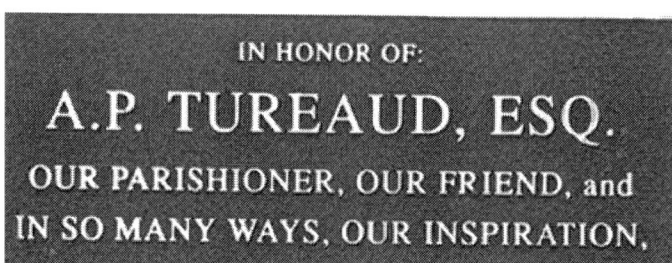

A. P. TUREAUD (TWO roe), formerly London Avenue, runs through the heart of the 7th Ward. It is named for civil rights lawyer Alexander Pierre Tureaud. His name is sometimes misspelled Tureau. He used his initials so people couldn't call him by his first name during the Jim Crow era. **See: Creole, Toulouse, Touro**

ARABIAN is a loving reference to someone who hails from Arabi, Louisiana. **See: Chalmation**

ARCADIA is the seat of Bienville Parish in the heart of Piney Hills Country - a few miles from where Bonnie & Clyde bit the dust. Arcadia means beautiful hills and is often confused with Acadia Parish.

ARK-LA-TEX is a four-state economic region, which includes Oklahoma, centered on the Shreveport-Bossier City metropolitan area.   It is seen in print in the following forms: Ark-La-Tex, Arklatex and ArkLaTex. Omitting Oklahoma really made the reference less cumbersome, didn't it? There is a city called Texarkana on the border of Texas and Arkansas.
See: Central Louisiana

ARTS DISTRICT is centered along Julia Street in the Warehouse District of New Orleans. It is popular for its abundance of art galleries and restaurants and is also ground zero for White Linen Night. **See: Dirty Linen Night, Warehouse District, White Linen Night**

ASH WEDNESDAY takes on a special meaning in New Orleans; in addition to its religious significance. At 12:01 am, Carnival comes to an abrupt end as mounted police parade down Bourbon Street to officially disperse the revelers, followed by an phalanx of garbage trucks. **See: Mardi Gras**

ATCHAFALAYA (uh CHAH fuh LYE yuh) is Choctaw for long river. The Atchafalaya Swamp in south-central Louisiana is a convergence of wetlands and the Atchafalaya River delta with the Gulf of Mexico.   Sometimes referred to as 'Chafalaya. The basin is traversed by a section of Interstate 10 known as the Atchafalaya Swamp Freeway. It is sometimes pronounced: (a chah fuh LYE yuh)   **See: Morganza, Old River Control Structure**

AUDUBON (AW duh bun) The street, park, zoo and state historic site are all named for the naturalist and painter John James Audubon. His name is often misspelled Audobon.
See: Monkey Hill, Riverview Park

AVERY ISLAND is a salt dome located in Iberia Parish surrounded on all sides by bayous. It is famous as the home of Tabasco Sauce. **See: Nutria, Tabasco**

AVONDALE (A vuhn dale) is a town in Jefferson Parish which is a local term synonymous with shipbuilding. The stressed A is short. Avondale was the plantation of George Waggaman. **See: Waggaman, West Bank**

AVOYELLES PARISH (uh VOILZ) forms the apex of the Cajun Triangle. It was named for the Avoyel Indian tribe which means flint people. **See: Cajun Heartland**

B IS FOR BANQUETTE

BABY BEN is the nickname for Benjamin Franklin Elementary School as opposed to Benjamin Franklin High.

BABY DOLLS This group of African American women has been seen around town on Mardi Gras since the early 1900s. They dress in satin bonnets and blouses carrying pacifiers and bottles presumably filled with liquor. They have also appeared as society women and even ladies of the evening. They often appear in the company of the Mardi Gras Indians in Tremé. **See: Mardi Gras Indians, Skull and Bone Gang**

BACCHUS (BAH kus) is one of Carnival's super krewes which started the tradition of celebrity monarchs. Bacchus is the god of wine and the celebrity should simply be referred to as Bacchus, not the King of Bacchus. **See: Barkus, Extravaganza, Krewe, Super Krewe**

BACK O'TOWN is an old reference to the area roughly bounded by Perdido, S. Liberty, Baronne and centered on S. Rampart Street. The area was famous for its honky-tonks and cheap bordellos. Known as the battlefield or Black Storyville, it was a very tough area in the early 1900s when Louis Armstrong grew up there. The area is very important to the history of jazz in New Orleans and is now home to the City Hall complex. **See: Storyville, Tango Belt**

BAGDAD is a small town in Grant Parish northwest of Alexandria which differs in spelling from Baghdad, Iraq.

BAG HEADS referred to disappointed Saints fans who were embarrassed to be seen in public at the Superdome. They wore Schwegmann's bags over their heads during home games in 1980 when the team went 1-15. Bag Heads are now extinct. **See: 'Aints, Bountygate, Schwegmann's Bag**

BALCONY Good examples of a New Orleans balcony can be found on the Napoleon House and Brennan's Restaurant featuring wrought iron brackets and railings. Not to be confused with a gallery. **See: Cast Iron, Gallery, Wrought Iron**

BALL refers to a formal Carnival affair, by invitation only, held by a krewe and presided over by the King and Queen. Also known as a bal masqué. **See: Court, Krewe Favor, Tableaux**

BANANAS FOSTER is not a nickname for former Gov. Mike Foster. Brennan's Restaurant is famous for this delectable dessert made with bananas, vanilla ice cream, butter, brown sugar, cinnamon, rum and banana liqueur which is dramatically set ablaze at the table. It was named for a family friend. **See: Café Brulot, Praline**

**ORLEANS STREET BANQUETTE
May 2005 - French Quarter**

BANQUETTE (BANK it) is the traditional New Orleans word for the sidewalk. In early New Orleans there were raised wooden platforms or embankments built so pedestrians could avoid the water and filth surrounding each city square or islet, especially in the original French Quarter. It is a reference one still hears today in many neighborhoods.
See: Neutral Ground

BARKUS The Krewe of Barkus is a Carnival parade for dogs and their owners. It is a play on words referring to the Bacchus parade. **See: Bacchus, City Bark, Endymeow, Mardi Gras**

BARONNE STREET (buh RONE) was named for Baronne de Carondelet, wife of the Spanish Governor. It is often misspelled Barrone. **See: Carondelet, Uptown**

BARQ'S (BARKS) is the local synonym for root beer. The Barq's Brothers Bottling Company makes several soft drink flavors, but is famous for its root beer. Due to the high caffeine content, it could not be labeled 'root beer' thus became known simply as Barq's. If you order a Barq's with your po-boy at a local restaurant, you will get a root beer - and a po-boy of course. **See: Dressed, Po-Boy, Red Drink**

BATON ROUGE (BAT uhn ROOZH) is the capital of Louisiana and is sometimes pronounced (ROOJ) in some neighborhoods. History suggests that the Houma and Bayou Goulas tribes marked their hunting boundaries with a pole stained with the blood of fish or animals. It was because of this red stick that French explorer Iberville christened the city, "le Baton Rouge." **See: Mer Rouge**

BATTLE OF THE BANDS refers to two events in New Orleans: The Krewe of Mid-City parade invites marching bands from across America to compete for the best band of Carnival. The annual Bayou Classic football game includes the "Battle of the Bands" on Friday of Thanksgiving week at the Superdome. **See: Mid-City, Superdome**

BATTURE DWELLERS refers to a small ramshackle community of buildings - part house, part camp - that sits between the levee and the river near Dakin Street and Monticello Avenue. These dwellers live in raised buildings with walkways built on stilts to avoid flooding. For a long time they lived rent and tax free since the area was considered part of the river.

BAYOU (BY you) is a slow-moving stream or creek. The word is thought to originate from the Choctaw word bayuk which means small stream. **See: Bonfouca, Sauvage, Segnette**

Quaint Essential New Orleans

BAYOU COUNTRY refers to a region stretching from Houston to Mobile with its center in New Orleans, Louisiana. **See: Gulf South**

BEAUREGARD (BOOR ri gahrd) Parish is named for Confederate General P. G. T. Beauregard. Congo Square was called Beauregard Square for many years. **See: Congo Square**

BEHRMAN (BER man) Street and Highway were named for former mayor of New Orleans, Martin Behrman. The name is generally misspelled Berhman or Bermann. **See: Shakspeare**

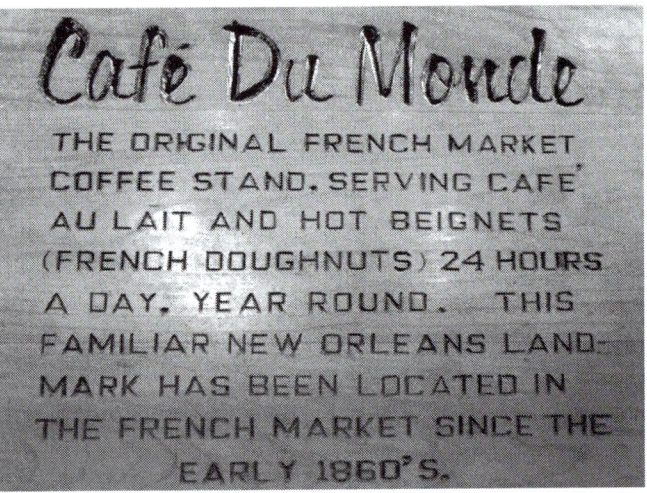

BEIGNET (ben YAY) is a French-style doughnut found at Café du Monde on Decatur Street. It is basically deep-fried dough, generously covered with confectioner's sugar. Locals never wear black when they eat there. If you don't know why, just try it. **See: Café au Lait, Café du Monde, Chicory, Decatur**

Quaint Essential New Orleans

BELLE CHASSE (BELL CHASE) means beautiful or good hunting. The city and Belle Chasse Highway, LA 23, are written as two words.

BELLECHASSE STREET located in Esplanade Ridge, was named for Joseph deVille Degoutin Bellechasse. It is written as one word.

And - there is that ignominious little sign that lurks on the West Bank Expressway. **See: Callender, West Bank**

BENSON BOOGIE is a charming but bizarre little dance performed by Saints owner Tom Benson along the Superdome sidelines near the end of victorious home games. He and his entourage create a "second line" with umbrellas decorated in black and gold. **See: 'Aints, Second Line**

BERMUDA TRIANGLE is a neighborhood reference to "McDonough" Park, a small triangular public park in Algiers bounded by Bermuda, Alix and Verret Streets. The park, by the way, was named for John McDonogh who owned much of the land in Old Algiers. The park officially bears the common misspelling of his name. **See: Algiers Point, McDonogh**

BERNADOTTE (BURN a dot) is a street near City Park named for Jean Baptiste Jules Bernadotte. It is often mispronounced: Bernadette - and often appears as such in print.

BIENVENUE (BYEN vuh new) This bayou forms the border between Orleans Parish and St. Bernard Parish near Paris Road and flows into Lake Borgne. It is often pronounced without the first N and misspelled likewise. **See: Bayou, Borgne, Green Bridge, Paris Road**

BIENVILLE (bee EN vil) Parish, as well as the city and street, were named for the founder of New Orleans. The French pronunciation of Jean-Baptiste Le Moyne de Bienville is (Zhan Bap teest Lay Moin day Bee en veel). **See: Driskill Mountain, Iberville**

BIG CHIEF "TOOTIE" MONTANA
Louis Armstrong Park - Tremé

BIG CHIEF Every Mardi Gras Indian tribe has a Big Chief to lead its procession on Mardi Gras or Super Sunday. He is often the oldest or most experienced member of the tribe. The late Allison 'Tootie" Montana is known as the Chief of Chiefs. **See: Mardi Gras Indians, Super Sunday**

BIG EASY is a tourism moniker for the slow, easy-going quality of life in New Orleans. Locals never use the term. However, try explaining that to the good folks who sponsor the annual Big Easy Awards. **See: Chocolate City, Crescent City, New Oileans**

Quaint Essential New Orleans

BIG SHOT In the hierarchy of the Zulu Social Aid and Pleasure Club, Big Shot precedes the King. No one can see the King of Zulu without seeing Big Shot first. There is also a Big Shot Cola based on the Zulu character. **See: Cold Drink, Zulu**

BISQUE (BISK) Crawfish bisque is a delicious Easter Sunday tradition in New Orleans and Louisiana. It is a rich soup made with crawfish and herbs served over rice and garnished with stuffed crawfish heads. **See: Crawfish, Étouffée**

BLACK PEARL does not refer to the ghost ship in *Pirates of the Caribbean.* It is a small neighborhood just west of Audubon Park which is also referred to as the Uptown Triangle. **See: Audubon**

BLUE BOOK Storyville's version of the Yellow Pages listed the names of the District's prostitutes, their addresses, racial backgrounds and even their prices. Today there would probably be an app for that. **See: Storyville**

Quaint Essential New Orleans

BLUE DOG is not a conservative New Orleans Democrat. It is the ubiquitous Loup Garou which appears in many of the paintings by Cajun artist George Rodrigue. **See: Green Bridge, Red Beans, White Kitchen, Yellow Fever**

BLUE ROOF refers to the blue tarps covering thousands of New Orleans homes after suffering wind damage from hurricane Katrina and rescue helicopters. **See: Katrina Tattoo**

BO BO (BOE boe) is a New Orleans childhood reference for a wound or bruise. Mom would kiss your bo bo and make it go away. **See: Grandma Beads**

BOEUF GRAS (BUHF graw) The fatted ox or bull is the symbol of the last meat eaten before Lent. A live boeuf gras once appeared in the Rex parade but it has been replaced with a papier-mâché one which smells much better. **See: Family Gras, Mardi Gras, Rex**

BOGALUSA (boe gah LOO sa) is a city in Washington Parish on the North Shore. The name Bogalusa is derived from the Bogue Lusa Creek which flows through the city. It is Choctaw for black creek or smoky waters. **See: Bogue Falaya, North Shore**

BOGUE CHITTO (boe gah CHEAT a) or (boeg CHEAT a) is a river in Washington Parish and part of the Pearl River floodplain. It is Choctaw for swift river.

BOGUE FALAYA (boe gah fuh LYE uh) or (boeg fuh LYE uh) is a river that flows through Covington, Louisiana. It is Choctaw for long river.

BONFOUCA (bon FOO ka) is a bayou near Slidell in St. Tammany Parish. Bonfouca was named after a local Indian chief.

BONNABEL (BON uh bul) This boulevard in Metairie is commonly pronounced this way. The family of Alfred Bonnabel insists it is pronounced: (bon uh BELL).

BONNET CARRÉ (BON ee KA ree) or (bon nay ka RAY) means square bonnet. In 1871, there was a disastrous break in the levee at this bonnet-shaped curve in the river. The Bonnet Carré Spillway was built here to control flooding. When opened, it relieves pressure on the levees allowing water from the Mississippi River to flow into Lake Pontchartrain and then into the Gulf of Mexico. **See: Morganza, Vieux Carré**

BOOTHVILLE-VENICE The towns, Boothville, Venice and Orchid in Plaquemines Parish are counted as a single town for census purposes. They are located just above Head of Passes on the Mississippi River. **See: Head of Passes, Plaquemines**

BOUCHERIE (BOO sha ree) is the butchering of a hog. It is a Cajun event to which family and neighbors are invited to attend. Everyone generally takes home some by-products of the butchering. **See: Cochon de Lait**

BOUDIN (BOO dan) Boudin Blanc is a highly seasoned sausage traditionally made with pork, rice, onions and spices encased in cooked pig intestines. Yum! Boudin Rouge has pig blood for added flavor. Double yum! It is available at the finest restaurants in Acadiana as well as every gas station. **See: Acadiana, Andouille**

BOUDREAUX (BOO dro) is a local surname made famous by Boudreaux's Butt Paste.

BOUILLABAISSE (BOO ya base) or (bwee yah BAYZ) is a Creole seafood stew made with red snapper or redfish and served with rice. The term means to stop or reduce the boil. **See: Courtbouillon**

BOULIGNY (BOO luh nee) is a neighborhood officially called Uptown and sits on the west side of Napoleon Avenue. It was known as Faubourg Bouligny named for the plantation of Louis Bouligny. **See: Derbigny, Faubourg, Marigny, Uptown**

BOUNY STREET in Algiers Point is named for Pierre Godefrey Bouny and is often misrepresented as Bounty Street. **See: Algiers Point**

BOUNTYGATE is the media nickname for the 2012 scandal involving Saints players and the alleged bounties being placed on opposing teams' players. The scandal resulted in severe penalties to the players, coaches and the Saints organization. I often wonder if anyone under the age of thirty understands why the suffix "gate" is attached to every scandal. **See: 'Aints, Bag Heads**

BOURG (BERG) is a small town located in Terrebonne Parish. **See: Faubourg**

BOURRÉ (BOO ray) is a gambling card game similar to spades and is popular in the Acadiana region of Louisiana. It is also known as Bouré and Boo-Ray. To misplay or lose is to "boo." It differs from bourrée which is a French dance.

BOUTTE (BOO TEE) is a town in St. Charles Parish known for its Alligator Festival.

BRAKE TAG is a New Orleans reference for an automobile inspection sticker. You have your car inspected at a "brake tag" station where you fail three times before passing.

BREAUX BRIDGE (BRO BRIJ) is a city in St. Martin Parish famous for its Crawfish Festival. The Louisiana Legislature officially designated Breaux Bridge as The Crawfish Capital of the World. **See: Crawfish, Étouffée**

BRIDGE CITY is a town in Jefferson Parish created during the construction of the Huey P. Long Bridge. It is located on the West Bank of the river. Bridge City is one of several cities billing itself as the Gumbo Capital of the World. **See: West Bank**

BROAD is a main city thoroughfare and part of Highway 90 that runs along the Gentilly Ridge. There is a sign on Gentilly Boulevard directing traffic to Broad Street, however the street signs actually say Broad Avenue.

Locals simply refer to it as Broad. Broad or Broadview once referred to the neighborhood which is now officially called Fairgrounds. **See: Fair Grounds, Fairgrounds, Tulane and Broad**

BROAD STREET OVERPASS is the common name for the South Broad Avenue Overpass where Broad crosses the Pontchartrain Expressway. In 1954, the name was officially changed to the Barnes Memorial Overpass - and I'll bet you did not know that. **See: Pontchartrain Expressway**

BROADMOOR (BROAD more) is a neighborhood in uptown New Orleans which is often misspelled Broadmore. **See: Crossroads, Uptown**

BROADWAY SOUTH is an economic development initiative designed to promote New Orleans as a theatrical destination for established Broadway musicals as well as previews of works in progress. It has led to the revival of the Saenger and Joy Theatres on Canal Street. **See: Canal Street, Hollywood South, Saenger Theatre**

BRUXELLES STREET (BRUCK CELLS) near Dillard University reflects the French spelling of Brussels, but is pronounced in our very own special way. **See: Cadiz, Milan**

BUCKTOWN This Metairie neighborhood, written as one word, is located on the opposite side of the 17th Street Canal from West End on the lakefront. It is famous for its seafood restaurants and harbor for shrimp boats. **See: Hammond Highway, Indian Beach, Metairie, West End**

BUFFALO ROAD There are no buffalo in New Orleans. Buffalo Road in the Little Woods neighborhood is named for the buffalo fish. **See: Choupique, Deers, Little Woods, Sheephead**

BUNNY FRIEND STREET When Bunny Friend died in the line of duty, the Friend family dedicated Bunny Friend Park in the St. Claude Neighborhood in his honor. The park is flanked by North and South Bunny Friend Streets.
I'm not sure what the sign painter was thinking ...

BURGUNDY STREET (ber GUN dee) This is the way locals have pronounced this street name since the beginning of time. However, it will only confuse the waiter if you order your wine this way. It was originally called Craps Street.
See: Cadiz, Clio, Milan

BURTHE STREET (BYOOTH) was named for Dominique Francois Burthe. The surrounding area, Faubourg Burtheville was a subdivision of the Burthe family's farmland. The origin of the pronunciation is uncertain. If you address your mail to Buth or Buthe Street, the mailman actually understands.

BYWATER is a neighborhood that runs along the Mississippi River and is part of the Upper Ninth Ward. The area was simply called downtown before World War II. A local business association wanted a catchy name for the area and sponsored a contest to name the neighborhood. A student from the former Nicholls High School came up with Bywater.
See: Governor Nicholls, Ninth Ward

NAUGHTY IN NEON
Bourbon Street – French Quarter

C IS FOR CAFÉ AU LAIT

CAC is an acronym for the Contemporary Arts Center on Camp Street which is housed in the old Katz & Besthoff (K&B) warehouse. **See: Arts District, K&B Purple**

CADIZ (KAY diz) Street in New Orleans is not pronounced like the city in Spain although it probably should be.
See: Milan

CAERNARVON (ka NAR von) is a rural area in St. Bernard Parish that is difficult to spell and pronounce. In 1927, the levee here was dynamited to prevent flooding in the city of New Orleans and we've never heard the end of it. Today it is the site of a fresh water diversion project attempting to stem coastal erosion. **See: Old River Control Structure**

CAFÉ AU LAIT (KA fay oh LAY) literally means coffee with milk. The coffee and chicory blend is dripped and the milk is scalded, not steamed, and mixed in a 1:1 ratio. The best in town: Café du Monde.
This term was also once used to refer to mulattoes or racially mixed people with a light brown skin tone.
See: Café du Monde, Chicory

CAFÉ BRULOT (KA fay broo LOW) is an after dinner coffee with spices, orange peel and liqueurs blended in a chafing dish and flamed at the table. It is a popular treat at Arnaud's Restaurant. **See: Bananas Foster**

CAFÉ DU MONDE (KA fay du MAHN) is a coffee shop located on Decatur Street in the French Quarter since 1862. It is famous for its café au lait and beignets. You can tell who the tourists are - they're the ones who wait for a table to be cleaned before sitting down. **See: Beignet, Café au Lait, Chicory**

CAJUN (KAY jun) is a derivative of the term Acadian. The French Acadians were exiled from British-controlled Nova Scotia and settled in Louisiana. They've had a tremendous influence on the food, music and culture of South Louisiana. **See: Coonass, Creole**

CAJUN CAVIAR See: Choupique

CAJUN COUNTRY is also known as the Cajun Triangle corresponding to the twenty-two parishes of Acadiana.

CAJUN HEARTLAND refers to the eight parishes which are the central portion of Acadiana initially settled by the majority of relocated Acadians. The parishes include Acadia, Evangeline, Iberia, Lafayette, St. Landry, St. Martin, St. Mary and Vermilion. **See: Evangeline, St. Mary, Vermilion**

CALCASIEU PARISH (KAL kuh shoo) is located in southwest Louisiana. Quelqueshu is the Attakapas word for crying eagle. The chief is supposed to have given a cry like an eagle when going into battle.

CALLE (KAHL yea) or (KAH yea) is Spanish for street. From 1762 to 1803, New Orleans was the capital of the Spanish Province of Louisiana. Rue Orleans became known as Calle d Orleans. **See: Rue**

CALLENDER FIELD Alvin Callender Field, the regional designation for the Naval Air Station-Joint Reserve Base, was named for World War I hero Alvin Callender. One should try to avoid the temptation to spell this: Calendar. **See: Belle Chasse, N'Awlins**

CALLIOPE STREET (KAL ee ope) is one of the Muse streets with a distinctly local pronunciation. Why use four syllables when three will do? However, the calliope aboard the Steamboat Natchez is still pronounced correctly, as well it should. **See: Clio, Euterpe, Melpomene, Terpsichore**

CALLIOPE PROJECTS (KAL ee ope)   Calliope was more recently known as the B. W. Cooper Apartments until it was evacuated after Hurricane Katrina. Now demolished, it has been reborn as mixed income units with the dreary name of Marrero Commons. **See: Marrero, Projects**

CALL-OUT refers to a special guest invited to participate in the first round of dances at a Carnival ball. They are generally given a "favor" by the anonymous krewe member who invited them to the dance. **See: Ball, Krewe Favor, Mardi Gras**

CAMELBACK is a variation of the shotgun house. This traditional style of housing in New Orleans has a single story in the front but two stories in the rear, presumably due to old property tax laws. **See: Shotgun**

CAMELIA STREET in New Orleans East is spelled with one L, unlike the Camellia Grill and Camellia Red Beans. **See: Red Beans and Rice, Wisteria**

CAMERON (KAM run) is a parish in southwest Louisiana famous for its unique cheniere topography. **See: Cheniere**

CANAL STREET is the widest street in New Orleans and was never a canal as originally intended. It was the dividing line that separated the Creole French Quarter from the Uptown Americans resulting in the term "neutral ground." Canal Street runs from the Mississippi River, the foot of Canal, to the cemeteries at City Park Avenue. From there to the lakefront it is called Canal Boulevard. **See: Cemeteries, Neutral Ground, Uptown**

CANNIBAL BURGER The Camellia Grill on Carrollton Avenue in New Orleans is famous for a lot of things, but this raw hamburger is one of its specialties. **See: Camelia, Riverbend**

CAPTAIN is the undisputed leader of a Carnival krewe who traditionally rides at the head of the parade on a horse. The identity of the captain is never revealed by traditional krewes. **See: Krewe**

CARENCRO (KER in cro) is a small town in Lafayette Parish. Legend has it that the name comes from the mispronunciation of carrion crow or vulture, common to the area. **See: Calcasieu**

CARNIVAL The Carnival season begins on January 6th - Twelfth Night - and ends on Mardi Gras. The word Carnival loosely translates to removal or farewell to flesh. The Carnival colors are purple (justice), gold (power) and green (faith). **See: King Cake, Mardi Gras, Rex**

CARONDELET STREET (ka RON duh LET) Don't bother trying to give this street in the CBD a fancy French pronunciation. Francisco Luis Hector, barón de Carondelet was born in Flanders and was the 5th Spanish Governor of Louisiana. **See: Baronne, CBD**

CARROLLTON AVENUE runs from City Park to the Mississippi River at St. Charles Avenue. This area was the independent town of Carrollton, named for William Carroll. It is now a neighborhood of New Orleans. The New Orleans and Carrollton Line is home to the St. Charles Streetcar.

Spelling can be tricky as you can see from this street sign. **See: Riverbend, Streetcar Barn**

CARROLLTON SPUR only refers to the section of the St. Charles Streetcar line that runs along Carrollton Avenue from Riverbend to S. Claiborne Avenue. Since the resurrection of the Canal Streetcar line, another spur was added along Carrollton Avenue in Mid-City to reach City Park, but it is known as the City Park spur. **See: Riverbend, Streetcar**

CASINO In New Orleans, the word Casino traditionally referred to a refreshment building in City Park ever since it was dedicated in 1913. It is sometimes called the old Casino or the Casino building, which literally means small house. It still stands in the park and houses the Morning Call coffeehouse. When you told someone to meet you at the Casino, there was never any question what you meant...until Harrah's came along! **See: Popp Fountain**

CAST IRON Tourist brochures tout the graceful wrought iron balconies of New Orleans and generally show a photo of the Pontalba Apartments. However, the Pontalba "galleries" overlooking Jackson Square are actually adorned with cast iron. Cast iron is poured into a mold. Wrought iron is formed by hand and can be found on the balcony of Brennan's Restaurant. **See: Balcony, Gallery, Wrought Iron**

Quaint Essential New Orleans

CATAHOULA (kat uh WHO luh) is a parish in Central Louisiana. It means big beloved lake. The Catahoula Leopard Dog was named after the parish and is now the Louisiana State Dog. **See: Louisiana State Seal**

CATAOUATCHE (kat uh WHO chee) This lake is in a marshy region about eight miles southwest of New Orleans. Often misspelled Catouatchie, or worse...

CAT ISLAND is a barrier island off the Gulf Coast of Mississippi named Isle-aux-Chats by early French explorers who thought the raccoons were cats - until they tried to pet one. It is easy to confuse this with the Cat Island National Wildlife Reserve in Louisiana.

CAT ISLAND National Wildlife Refuge is located near the town of St. Francisville in West Feliciana Parish. The refuge was established to conserve, restore and manage native forested wetland habitats. It is home to the world's largest bald cypress tree.

CAT ISLAND, LA is a small barrier island in Cat Bay, Plaquemines Parish. The Pelican rookeries located here were the first casualties in the BP oil spill of 2010. **See: New Oileans**

CAUSEWAY The bridge that crosses Lake Pontchartrain connecting Metairie to Mandeville is officially called The Lake Pontchartrain Causeway. It consists of two parallel spans and is still listed as the longest bridge in the world at just under twenty-four miles. Local traffic reporters insist on calling it the Causeway Bridge - I call it redundant. Not to be confused with the Pontchartrain Expressway or the Twin Spans.
See: Highway 11 Bridge, Metairie, North Shore, Twin Spans

CAVELIER DRIVE in the Michoud area of New Orleans is actually spelled correctly. It is named for the explorer, René Robert Cavelier, Sieur de La Salle. **See: Michoud**

CBD is an acronym for the Central Business District. It was historically called The American Quarter. In its early days it was known as Faubourg St. Mary. It is also called Uptown since it is located on the upriver side of Canal Street from the Creole French Quarter. **See: Faubourg, Neutral Ground**

CCC is the acronym for the Crescent City Connection and the Crescent City Classic. The Connection is the new name for the Greater New Orleans Bridge over the Mississippi River.

The Crescent City Classic is an annual 10K foot race that starts in the French Quarter and ends with a big party in City Park. **See: Crescent City Connection**

CDBG is the acronym for Community Development Block Grants; a federal program providing funds to Louisiana for local distribution to private and public organizations for Katrina recovery...at least in theory. **See: LRA**

CELEBRATION IN THE OAKS This annual holiday celebration in City Park runs from November until New Years.
See: Mr. Bingle

CEMETERIES is a reference to the intersection of Canal Street, Canal Boulevard and City Park Avenue. The term actually appears on the destination panels of streetcars even if no one is in any hurry to get there. In the play, *A Streetcar Named Desire*, Blanche says, "They told me to take a streetcar named Desire, and then transfer to one called Cemeteries ..."

The intersection is at the convergence of no less than eight historic cemeteries. They are an important part of the culture of New Orleans due to their unique above-ground architecture. They are often called cities of the dead. Common misspellings "cemetary" and "cemetaries" should be avoided.
See: All Saints Day, Canal Street, NOPSI, Oven

DESTINATION: CEMETERIES
Canal Street & City Park Avenue - Mid-City

CENTRAL LOCK UP is a holding pen operated by the Criminal Sheriff's Office where the New Orleans Police drop off vagrants, DWI arrestees and prostitutes, where they linger for decades until someone posts bond. **See: OPP, Tulane and Broad**

CENTRAL LOUISIANA, sometimes abbreviated CenLa, is known as the Crossroads region. Central Louisiana includes the following ten parishes: Allen, Beauregard, Catahoula, Concordia, Grant, La Salle, Natchitoches, Rapides, Sabine and Vernon. **See: Crossroads, Natchitoches, Rapides**

CHACKBAY (SHAK bay) is a town in Lafourche Parish and is ground zero for the annual Louisiana Gumbo Cook-Off. **See: Lafourche**

CHALMATION is an amusing term used to refer to a resident of Chalmette. Well – at least I *think* it's amusing. **See: Arabian, Chalmette Nikes**

CHALMETTE (SHALL MET) is the parish seat of St. Bernard and home to the Chalmette Battlefield and National Cemetery. It was here that Andrew Jackson defeated the British at the Battle of New Orleans in 1815. Also known as Port Chalmette. **See: da Parish, Green Bridge, Paris Road, St. Tammanard**

CHALMETTE NIKES are those ubiquitous white shrimp boots worn by many fishermen who live, work and fish in St. Bernard Parish. It is costume de rigueur at Rocky & Carlo's. Sometimes called Chalmette Reeboks. **See: Wop Salad**

CHANDELEUR ISLANDS (SHAN duh LURE) Often mispronounced "Chandelier," the Chandeleur Islands are a crescent-shaped archipelago in the Gulf of Mexico forming the easternmost point in Louisiana. Also known as Islas de la Chandeleur. **See: Grand isle, Isles Dernières**

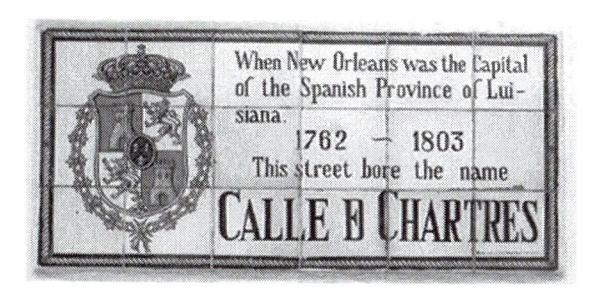

> When New Orleans was the Capital of the Spanish Province of Luisiana.
> 1762 — 1803
> This street bore the name
> **CALLE D CHARTRES**

CHARTRES (CHAR ters) Street, in the French Quarter, is named for the Duc de Chartres. When you get right down to it we probably say (CHAW tuz)! Never spell it Charters and never pronounce it (char TREZ). **See: Decatur**

CHAURICE is a spicy pork sausage seasoned with a variety of vegetables and used primarily in Creole cooking and some Cajun dishes. It can also be served as a pan-fried side dish with red beans and rice. **See: Andouille, Red Beans & Rice, Tasso**

CHAZ FEST is a home-grown music festival staged on the Wednesday between Jazz Fest weekends on the Truck Farm in Bywater. It is a popular venue for local musicians since 2006 when washboard player Chaz Leary was bumped by Jazz Fest organizers. **See: Bywater, Jazz Fest**

Chef Menteur Hwy

CHEF MENTEUR (SHEF men TOUR) One thing is certain - this is not a famous Creole cook! Chef Menteur Pass, or Chef Pass, is a narrow waterway connecting Lake Pontchartrain with Lake Borgne. The stretch of Highway 90 from Indian Village to the state line is called Chef Menteur Highway, or simply Chef Highway. It is believed to be a Native American term for "big liar" or "chief liar" due to the unpredictable current associated with the Pass. **See: Indian Village, Lake Borgne, Rigolets**

CHENIERE (sha NEAR) is a sandy ridge with live oak trees found along the coastal marshlands of Cameron Parish. Chene is French for oak and early French settlers used the term Cheniere for an oak grove. Spelling varies as in Cheniere Caminada and the city of Cheniere. It is also spelled without the final 'e' as in Grand Chenier, Little Chenier, Chenier Perdue, as well as musician Clifton Chenier. Some residents of Cheniere, Louisiana say (SHEN nee) for the city and Lake Cheniere. **See: Cameron, Dueling Oaks, Spanish Moss**

CHICORY (CHICK or ee) is an herb with blue flowers; basically a weed. The roots are baked, ground and used as a coffee extender and flavoring; a practice that is said to have been started by the French during their civil war. You generally assume that coffee and chicory will be served at most New Orleans restaurants. This is not true for national chains. The alternative is pure coffee, referred to as regular coffee. **See: Café au Lait, Café du Monde**

CHICKEN KING is a local reference given to the late Al Copeland who founded the ubiquitous Popeye's Fried Chicken outlets beginning with a humble little restaurant in Arabi. Popeye's Chicken is traditional parade food. "Love that chicken!" **See: Arabian**

CHOCOLATE CITY

A Politician's Faux-pas Inspired This Deliciously Satirical Chocolate Ice Cream With White Chocolate Chips.

16 oz. (437 mL)

CHOCOLATE CITY is the controversial reference to New Orleans made in a post-Katrina speech by Mayor Ray Nagin. It is now a flavor produced by the New Orleans Ice Cream Company. **See: Big Easy, Crescent City, New Oileans**

CHOUPIQUE (SHOO pick), the ugliest fish in Louisiana waters, was called shupik by the Choctaw Indians and it means filthy. Some people refer to it as a cypress bass. In other parts of the country it is known as a mudfish or bowfin. It is the source of a local delicacy called "Cajun Caviar." Choupique is also the name of small towns located in Evangeline and Calcasieu Parishes, as well as an excellent Cajun band.
See: Buffalo, Calcasieu, Sheephead

CHURCH KEY I remember attending family crab boils and watching my parents open a cold can of Dixie Beer with what they called a "church key." This single piece of metal had a pointed end for cans and a bottle opener on the other end. It was actually developed by the American Can Company. The American Can Company in New Orleans is now the American Can Apartments. **See: Dixie, Jax Brewery**

CITY BARK is the new dog park located in City Park. **See: Barkus**

CLAIBORNE BRIDGE is the common reference to the vertical lift bridge where Claiborne Avenue crosses the Industrial Canal connecting the Upper and Lower Ninth Wards of New Orleans. It is officially named the Judge William Seeber Bridge. **See: Industrial Canal**

CLIO (KLI oh) is one of the Muse streets with a distinctly local pronunciation. The old Clio streetcar line was often referred to as C-L-TEN because the destination panel read: CLIO. **See: Calliope, Euterpe, Melpomene**

CLOUET (KLEW it) is a street in Bywater named for the DeClouet family but without the fancy pronunciation.
See: Bywater

COCHON DE LAIT (KO SHON da LAY) is a Cajun family cooking event that involves the roasting of an entire suckling pig in a wire rotisserie cage over pecan and hickory wood. A cochon de lait festival is held annually in the small Cajun town of Mansura. **See: Avoyelles, Boucherie, Boudin, Cajun, Cracklins**

COCKTAIL SAUCE is red dipping sauce usually served with peeled, boiled shrimp in a cocktail glass called...a "shrimp cocktail." It traditionally contains ketchup, lemon juice, horseradish, Worcestershire sauce, Tabasco and salt.
See: Remoulade

COCODRIE (KO cuh dree) or (KO ko dree) is a small community in south Terrebonne Parish. It is Cajun French for alligator. **See: Carencro, Terrebonne**

COCONUT BEACH is a popular sand volleyball complex once located in West End until hurricane Katrina. The complex recently relocated to Kenner. **See Indian Beach, Lincoln Beach**

COCONUT BILL The Zulu coconut, or "golden nugget," is one of the most treasured Mardi Gras throws. After several injuries and lawsuits the state legislature passed Bill #SB188, the Coconut Bill, excluding Zulu from liability as long as the coconuts are handed out. New Orleans is probably the only place in the world where having coconuts and cabbages thrown at you is considered a compliment.
See: St. Patrick's Day, Throw, Zulu

COLD DRINK (KOLE drink) is a New Orleans reference for a soft drink or cola. **See: Barq's, Red Drink**

COMUS See: Mistick Krewe of Comus

CONFEDERATE MUSEUM is located on Camp Street. The museum has become politically correct and now bills itself as the Civil War Museum and Confederate Memorial Hall. **See: Dixie**

CONGO SQUARE

Congo Square is in the "vicinity" of a spot which Houmas Indians used before the arrival of the French for celebrating their annual corn harvest and was considered sacred ground. The gathering of enslaved African vendors in Congo Square originated as early as the late 1740's during Louisiana's French colonial period and continued during the Spanish colonial era as one of the city's public markets. By 1803, Congo Square had become famous for the gatherings of enslaved Africans who drummed, danced, sang and traded on Sunday afternoons. By 1819, these gatherings numbered as many as 500 to 600 people. Among the most famous dances were the Bamboula, the Calinda and the Congo. These African cultural expressions gradually developed into Mardi Gras Indian traditions, the Second line and eventually New Orleans jazz and rhythm and blues.

CONGO SQUARE WAS LISTED ON THE NATIONAL REGISTER OF HISTORIC PLACES ON JANUARY 26, 1993.

CONGO SQUARE is an area adjacent to Louis Armstrong Park just in front of the Municipal Auditorium in Tremé. It was the original town square of Tremé and once called, "Place des Nègres." The square is famous for its history of African dance and music. Though officially renamed Beauregard Square in the early 20th Century, it is now officially referred to as Congo Square. It was the original site of the Jazz Fest.
See: Beauregard, Jazz Fest, Tremé

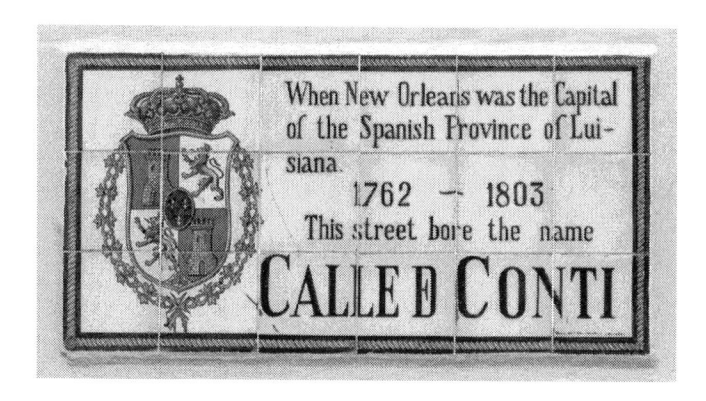

> When New Orleans was the Capital of the Spanish Province of Luisiana.
> 1762 — 1803
> This street bore the name
> **CALLE D CONTI**

CONTI (KON tye) is a street in the French Quarter. If you call the Musée Conti Wax Museum in New Orleans to get information, they answer: "Musée (kon TEE) on (KON tye) Street." **See: Tonti**

COONASS is a reference to a Cajun which is considered an insult by older Cajuns; but it often depends on how it is used. Flamboyant former Governor Edwin Edwards openly referred to himself as a Coonass. The term is most likely derived from the French noun "conasse" which refers to someone who is inept or does stupid things. Perhaps Bobby "Cajun Cannon" Hebert can best explain: "A Coonass can call a Coonass a Coonass, but it might not always be a good idea to call a Coonass a Coonass if you're not a Coonass yourself." Eloquent. **See: Cajun, Fast Eddie**

COTE BLANCHE ISLAND is an "island" or salt dome located in St. Mary Parish. It was settled by hurricane refuges in 1893 who painted their homes white and became known as a "village of white houses." **See: Avery Island, Five Islands, St. Mary**

COURIR DE MARDI GRAS (ku REE) is French for "Fat Tuesday Run." This traditional Mardi Gras event occurs in several Cajun communities across rural Louisiana. Popular practice includes masking and wearing costumes, ignoring social conventions, dancing, alcohol, begging and feasting. Sounds like an average day in my neighborhood. **See: Cajun, Mardi Gras**

COURT refers to a Carnival krewe's king, queen, dukes and debutante maids. They are officially presented at the krewe's annual Carnival ball. **See: Ball, Mardi Gras, Meeting of the Courts**

COURTBOUILLON (KOO bee yahn) or (KOO boo yahn) is a well-seasoned stew, beginning with a roux, made with redfish or catfish filets, tomatoes, onions, mixed vegetables and spices. This is a traditional meal for Friday evenings during the Lenten season. **See: Bouillabaisse, Roux**

COURT OF TWO SISTERS is a restaurant on Royal Street which was named after two sisters from an aristocratic Creole family. Emma and Bertha Camors operated a notions shop at this location in the late 19th Century. Not to be confused with the Pavilion of the Two Sisters in City Park or Two Sisters Restaurant. **See: Creole, Pavilion of the Two Sisters**

COUTURIE FOREST (koo TOUR ee ay) and Arboretum Trail is a thirty-three acre preserve in City Park named for businessman Rene Couturie. **See: Laborde Lookout**

COWAN (KOW WAHN) is the Cajun word for turtle, specifically the giant alligator snapping turtle which is the source of most turtle meat for Cajun and Creole cooking. **See: Cajun**

CRAB TRAP What we call a crab trap is technically a crab pot. It is a large square trap made of chicken wire. Built with an upper and lower chamber; it traps crabs with the help of their unbelievable stupidity. The lower chamber is baited and the crab swims upward and becomes trapped in the "parlor."
See: Dead Men's Fingers, Loaded She

CRACKLINS Grattons (grah TAWN), or cracklins, is Cajun snack food. Basically, strips of seasoned pork with skin, fat and meat attached are rendered for 90 minutes or so in 250 degree lard which removes some fat. They are then flash fried at 400 degrees to produce the crunchy texture. Salt to taste and make them even healthier. It is a byproduct of the boucherie. **See: Boucherie, Cochon de Lait**

CRAWFISH (KRAW fish) The standard dictionary spelling and pronunciation is "crayfish." However, ordering boiled (KRAY fish) in a local seafood market is the same as having TOURIST stamped on your forehead. You may occasionally hear locals refer to them as mudbugs; but not crawdads. They are listed as ecrevisses (ay kray VEEZ) on some fancy French menus. **See: Bisque, Breaux Bridge, Étouffée, Melts**

CREOLE (CREE yole)   There are as many definitions of Creole as there are recipes for gumbo. The common element of all definitions is: a descendent of early settlers born in southeast Louisiana.   Let's just agree that New Orleans is a Creole city; it is not Cajun, being geographically separate from Cajun Country.   The Seventh Ward is considered to be the quintessential Creole neighborhood in New Orleans. Creole cuisine and culture originated in Louisiana (centered in New Orleans) and blends French, Spanish, French Caribbean, African and American influences. The term is now used to describe everything from local architecture to tomatoes. Dooky Chase restaurateur, Leah Chase, was cooking Creole gumbo on a talk show when the host asked her what makes this dish Creole. Her answer: "Because I'm cooking it!" Enough said. **See: Cajun, Gumbo, Holy Trinity**

CREOLE CREAM CHEESE   A product of France, Creole Cream Cheese has been a New Orleans culinary tradition for over 150 years. The Cream Cheese Woman was a common sight on the early streets of the French Quarter. It is best described as a combination of cottage cheese and sour cream. Local dairies produced it for many years until state health officials affected its availability. Creole Cream Cheese is a breakfast treat sprinkled with sugar, cream or syrup; often mixed with fresh fruit. It is rarely found outside Louisiana or even in New Orleans for that matter. However, there has been a recent resurgence of Creole Cream Cheese in some local restaurants and supermarkets.

CREOLE MUSTARD Stone-ground brown mustard is also called hot mustard, differentiating it from yellow mustard. It is a common option for po-boys and an ingredient in remoulade sauce. **See: Dressed, Po-Boy, Remoulade**

CRESCENT CITY is the common and locally acceptable nickname for New Orleans since the city was founded along the sharp bend in the Mississippi River. **See: Big Easy, Chocolate City**

CRESCENT CITY CONNECTION The CCC, formerly the Greater New Orleans Bridge, is the official name of the twin cantilever bridges that cross the Mississippi River connecting New Orleans to the West Bank. Television traffic reporters often call it the Crescent City Connection Bridge, presumably to fill time or just to aggravate the life out of me. **See: Algiers Point, CCC, East Bank, West Bank**

CRETE (KREET) Street, which traverses the Fairgrounds neighborhood, is not named after the Mediterranean island. It is French for ridge; specifically the ridge that was formed along Bayou Gentilly. **See: Broad, Fairgrounds, Gentilly Ridge**

CROSSROADS is a neighborhood reference to the area where Broad Street intersects with Washington Avenue, Toledano Street, Fontainebleau Drive and Napoleon Avenue. It is the nexus of Gert Town, Zion City, Broadmoor, Marlyville-Fontainebleau and the Hoffman Triangle neighborhoods. **See: Broad, Fontainebleau, Gert Town, Napoleon**

Quaint Essential New Orleans

CUT OFF is a town on Bayou Lafourche in Lafourche Parish. It is named after a canal used in the exploration and drilling of the oil and natural gas fields. Cut Off is the home of the annual Cajun Heritage Festival. **See: Lafourche**

CUTOFF is a community in Algiers near the Old Aurora neighborhood. Cutoff is written as one word. **See: Algiers Point**

SACRED COWS
Brown's Velvet Dairy - Central City
July 2004

ELIZABETH'S BILL OF FARE
601 Gallier Street - Bywater
Artist - Dr. Bob

D IS FOR DESIRE

D'ABADIE (DA ba dee) Street is named for Jean-Jacques Blaise d'Abbadie, French Governor of Louisiana from 1763-1765, is officially misspelled or they just ran out of Bs for the street tiles. **See: Onzaga**

DANNEEL STREET (da NEEL) When S. Rampart Street fell into disrepute, the street was renamed for Rudolph Danneel. It is often misspelled: Daneel.

DANZIGER BRIDGE (DAN zig er) is named after Alfred Danziger. This bridge on Chef Menteur Highway, crossing the Industrial Canal, is often mispronounced and misspelled "Danzinger." **See: Chef Menteur, Claiborne Bridge, Green Bridge, Industrial Canal, Seabrook Bridge**

da PARISH Of all the parishes in Louisiana, only St. Bernard has the distinction of being referred to as "da Parish." **See: Chalmation, Parish, Paris Road**

DAUPHINE STREET (daw FEEN) runs through the French Quarter all the way to the east Orleans Parish line. **See: Chartres, Decatur**

DEAD MAN'S CURVE is a treacherous little bend in Highway 90 just south of the Rigolets and Fort Pike near the scene of actress Jayne Mansfield's deadly car accident in 1967. **See: Rigolets, White Kitchen**

DEAD MEN'S FINGERS When opening and cleaning a boiled crab, you remove the shriveled, spongy, grey finger-like gills or "dead men" so you can get to the spicy crab meat. **See: Crab Trap, Loaded She**

DECATUR (da KAY ter) Street is named after Commodore Stephen Decatur and runs through the French Quarter. It was formerly known as Levee Street and is often misspelled Decater. **See: Chartres**

DEERS STREET The word deer, of course, is both singular and plural so no one seems to know why this Gentilly street has taken on this peculiar spelling. As they say, "only in New Orleans." **See: Sheephead**

DELACROIX ISLAND (DEL uh crow) is a settlement of Los Isleños along Bayou Terre aux Boeufs in St. Bernard Parish. Originally referred to as La Isla de la Croix or the island belonging to Francois du Suau de la Croix. It is referred to by locals as "the Island." **See: da Parish, End of the World, Isleños**

DELCAMBRE (del KAHMB) is a small town directly on the Vermilion/Iberia Parish line that hosts an annual Shrimp Festival. **See: Vermilion**

DELGADO (del GA dough) Isaac Delgado's name appears on a street and a trade school. The Delgado Art Museum in City Park is now known as NOMA. **See: NOMA**

DELTA refers to three distinct regions along the Mississippi River: The **Mississippi River Delta** is the area of land built up by alluvium deposited by the Mississippi River as it enters the Gulf of Mexico. The **Mississippi Delta** is the home of the musical form known as the Delta blues. It stretches from Memphis to Vicksburg and from the Mississippi River to the Yazoo River. The village of **Delta**, Louisiana, sits on the Mississippi River just across from Vicksburg. **See: Head of Passes, Pilottown**

DEN This is not a meeting place for Boy Scouts, but a warehouse where a Carnival krewe builds and stores its parade floats during the off season. **See: Krewe, Mardi Gras**

DERBIGNY (DER buh nee) Street was named after Louisiana Gov. Pierre Derbigny. The G is silent.
See: Bouligny, Marigny

DE SAIX (duh SAY) is a boulevard, traffic circle and a neighborhood (De Saix Place) in the Fairgrounds District of New Orleans.

Most 7th and 8th Ward residents proudly pronounce it (DEE sacks). **See: Fair Grounds, Fairgrounds**

Quaint Essential New Orleans

ALLEMANDS (days AL uh mahn)   Parts of the city es Allemands rest in both Lafourche and St. Charles Parishes. It is French for "of the Germans" and is the Catfish Capital of the Universe.   Sometimes pronounced: (days AHL MAHN) **See: River Parishes, German Coast**

DESIRE STREET is a famous New Orleans street named for Desirée Montreuil. A poor translation into English produced Desire. I guess *A Streetcar Named Desirée* just wouldn't have sounded the same! It is also the name of a neighborhood in the Upper Ninth Ward, a former housing development and, of course, a bar on Bourbon Street.
See: Cemeteries, Streetcar

DESIRE PROJECTS   This former housing development in the St. Claude neighborhood was once known at the Abundance Projects. **See: Projects**

DEVIL'S ELBOW was a dangerous curve in Bayou St. John which was bypassed after the Civil War with the creation of Park Island providing safer navigation between Lake Pontchartrain and Back O'Town. **See: Back O'Town, Park Island**

DIRTY D was an unflattering reference to the former Desire House Development. **See: Projects**

DIRTY LINEN NIGHT is the French Quarter's answer to White Linen Night, held the second Saturday in August. Art lovers can stroll down Royal Street wearing their soiled linens from the previous weekend and sip dirty martinis and eat dirty rice. Not to be outdone, there is now a Filthy Linen Night in Marigny. **See: White Linen Night**

DIRTY RICE is a Cajun pilaf–style rice dish. It contains small pieces of chicken livers or giblets cooked with bell peppers, celery and onions. **See: Holy Trinity, Jambalaya**

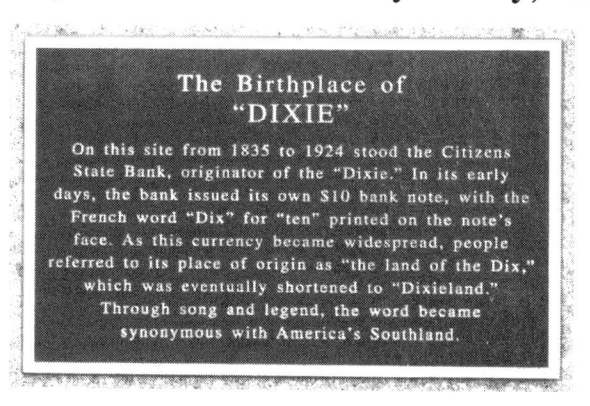

> **The Birthplace of "DIXIE"**
> On this site from 1835 to 1924 stood the Citizens State Bank, originator of the "Dixie." In its early days, the bank issued its own $10 bank note, with the French word "Dix" for "ten" printed on the note's face. As this currency became widespread, people referred to its place of origin as "the land of the Dix," which was eventually shortened to "Dixieland." Through song and legend, the word became synonymous with America's Southland.

DIXIE is a nickname for the Southern United States. Dixie is also a famous local beer once brewed on Tulane Avenue. There is a town called Dixie in Caddo Parish.
See: Confederate Museum

COUSIN'S BEER PARLOR
North Rampart Street - Bywater
August 1985

Quaint Essential New Orleans

DIXIELAND The term Dixieland is now used almost exclusively in New Orleans to refer to Dixieland Jazz, one of the earliest styles of jazz music. **See: Jazz Fest, Jazz Funeral**

DOCK BOARD The Port of New Orleans is overseen by the Board of Commissioners of the Port of New Orleans. It is simply referred to as the Dock Board. **See: Sewerage & Water Board**

DO DO (dough dough) To make do do means to sleep or go to sleep; related to the Cajun French reference fais do do. Do do comes from the French verb dormir - to sleep. It is sometimes hyphenated as: do-do. **See: Fais Do Do**

DON'T EAT THE DEAD ONES is a strangely worded warning to novices while eating boiled crawfish. When a live crawfish hits the boil, its tail curls up. The ones that have straight tails were probably dead before they hit the water and we don't eat those. **See: Crawfish, Suck da heads**

DORGENOIS (DER zhen wah) is a street named for Francois J. D'Orgenois, U.S. Marshal.

DOUBLOON is a silver dollar-size coin made of aluminum and thrown to parade crowds. They are dated and bear the Carnival krewe's insignia and parade theme. The tradition was started by the Rex organization in 1960. **See: Rex, Throw**

DOUBLOON REFLEX There is actually a local phenomenon known as the "doubloon reflex." When we hear a doubloon, or anything metallic, hit the cement (SEE ment) our foot automatically stomps on the ground in front of us to prevent anyone else from getting it. **See: Pair of Beads**

DOUGLASS The former Francis T. Nicholls High School was often misspelled with one L. It was eventually changed to Frederick Douglass High School which is often misspelled with one S. **See: Gov. Nicholls**

DRESSED If you want your po-boy to include all the necessary condiments such as pickles, lettuce, tomatoes and mayonnaise, you order it dressed. Known elsewhere as "the works." If you want mustard, you must specify yellow or hot (Creole). Dressed also refers to a soft-shell crab that has had its eyes and gills removed in preparation for frying or broiling. **See: Creole Mustard, Mynez, Po-Boy, Soft Shell Crab**

DRESSIN' ROOM No, this is not a place where they garnish your po-boy. It is our polite way of saying bathroom.

DREUX (DREW) Avenue was named for the Dreux brothers who owned and developed the vast tract now called Gentilly. It is often misspelled Dreaux. **See: Gentilly Ridge**

DUELING OAKS is the notorious spot located in City Park where gentlemen settled their "affaires d'honneur" with pistols or swords. It is still referred to as the Dueling Oaks even though one oak lost a duel with a hurricane many years ago. **See: Cheniere, Spanish Moss**

DUELING OAK
Allard Plantation - City Park
March 2005

DUFOSSAT STREET (DOO faucet) A street in Uptown New Orleans which is often pronounced this way.

DUNCAN PLAZA Named for Brooke Duncan, the plaza is the green space between the Public Library and City Hall in the CBD. It was city planner Duncan who developed the idea of a Civic Plaza for New Orleans. **See: CBD, Back O'Town**

DUTCH ALLEY is located along the 900 block of N. Peters Street in the French Quarter and home to several art galleries and sculptures. It was named after Mayor Earnest "Dutch" Morial. Just follow Dumaine Street to the River.
See: Moonwalk, Pirates Alley

E IS FOR ÉTOUFFÉE

EARHART BOULEVARD (AIR hart) runs through Orleans Parish and changes to Earhart Expressway as it passes through Jefferson Parish. By the way, it was named for public utilities commissioner, Fred Earhart - not Amelia.
See: Airline Highway

EAST BANK The East Bank includes most of the New Orleans metropolitan area including suburbs that are situated on the eastern side of the Mississippi River. Due to the curve in the river, the East Bank is, for the most part, north of the West Bank. Trust me. **See: West Bank**

EGANIA STREET in the Lower Ninth Ward was named for a prominent New Orleans family.

Some of the street tiles are prominently misspelled.

ELEONORE STREET Eleanor Smith Hurst, wife of Cornelius Hurst, has her name forever misspelled on the streets of New Orleans. Their children, Arabella & Joseph, had better luck. **See: Hennessy**

ELK PLACE   The first block of Loyola Avenue, south of Canal Street, is called Elk Place for the former Elks Home located there.

Elk Place should always be written without an S except, apparently, on this sign in the 100 block. **See: Pirates Alley**

EMPEROR OF THE WORLD   Ernie K-Doe - who else! **See: All Saints Day**

END OF THE WORLD   If you make the trek down Highway 39 through St. Bernard Parish, to Highway 46 at Reggio, and then onto Highway 300 down to Delacroix, it seems like you have traveled to the end of the world. In fact, there was a marina there called the "End of the World Marina." Venice, Louisiana also claims the nickname, "The end of the World."   **See: Boothville-Venice, da Parish, Delacroix**

ENDYMION (en DIM ee on) is one of Carnival's super krewes which holds its parade on the Saturday evening before Mardi Gras. **See: Extravaganza**

ENDYMEOW The Krewe of Endymeow is an all feline Carnival krewe. Krewe members hold their annual bal masqué with the assistance of their human companions. **See: Ball, Barkus**

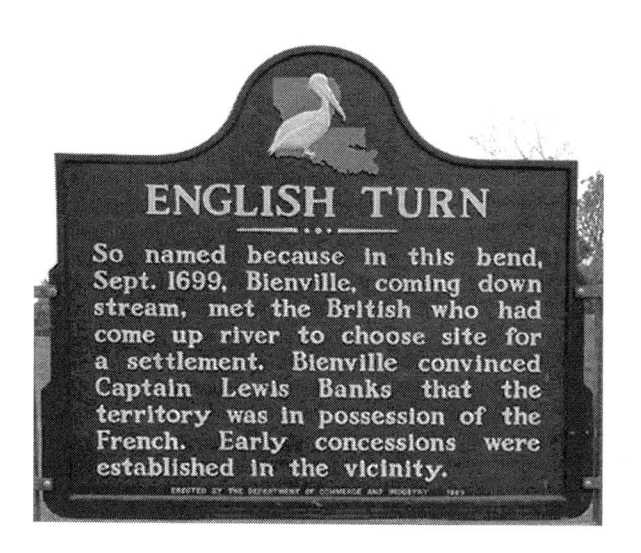

> **ENGLISH TURN**
>
> So named because in this bend, Sept. 1699, Bienville, coming down stream, met the British who had come up river to choose site for a settlement. Bienville convinced Captain Lewis Banks that the territory was in possession of the French. Early concessions were established in the vicinity.

ENGLISH TURN is a bend in the Mississippi River about 10 miles southeast of New Orleans. It is also an official neighborhood of New Orleans located on the lower coast of Algiers on the West Bank also known as New Aurora.
See: Dead Man's Curve

ESPLANADE AVENUE (es pla NADE) forms the eastern border of the French Quarter; once a city commons dividing the Quarter from Faubourg Marigny. Esplanade runs from the Mississippi River to Bayou St. John. The neighborhood from Rampart Street to the bayou is known as the Esplanade Ridge. There is also a West Esplanade Avenue in Jefferson Parish.
See: Bayou, Faubourg, Marigny

ÉTOUFFÉE (AY too FAY) This is a method of cooking by smothering seafood or meat in chopped vegetables, especially the holy trinity, and also includes tomatoes. The French word means to braise or cook slowly in a closed pot. Crawfish and shrimp étouffée are served over rice and are classic Louisiana dishes. **See: Crawfish, Gumbo, Holy Trinity**

EUPHROSINE (YOU fra zeen) is a street in Gert Town named for Euphrosyne, the Grace of Mirth. This is how we choose to pronounce and spell it. **See: Gert Town**

EUTERPE STREET (YOU terp)   The Greek Muse of Music is always pronounced this way in New Orleans.
See: Calliope, Clio, Melpomene

EXTRAVAGANZA Super Krewes end their parades at the Morial Convention Center or the Mercedes-Benz Superdome where they throw formal parties and supper dances. Unlike a traditional bal masqué, the public can purchase tickets to these events. Extravaganza has become a generic term for all of these events. For the record, they are called the Endymion 'Extravaganza,' the 'Orpheuscapade,' as well as the Bacchus 'Rendezvous.' **See: Bacchus, Mardi Gras, Super Krewe**

MOTHER GOOSE
Storyland - City Park - 2006

F IS FOR FLAMBEAUX

FAIR GROUNDS JOCKEY
Gentilly Boulevard - Fairgrounds

FAIR GROUNDS Historically referred to as the New Orleans Fair Grounds, this race track should be spelled as two words. It is now owned by Churchill Downs and is officially called the Fair Grounds Race Course & Slots. It is located in the neighborhood known as Fairgrounds which is one word. Racing season starts on Thanksgiving Day. **See: Jazz Fest**

FAIRGROUNDS The Fairgrounds neighborhood is in the Gentilly district and is one word. It was once known as Broad or Broadview. **See: Broad, Gentilly Ridge**

FAIS DO DO or FAIS DO-DO (FAY dough dough) is the name of a Cajun dance party usually held after the children have gone to sleep. Fais do do basically means to make do do or go to sleep. **See: Do Do**

KING GAMBRINUS
Falstaff Brewery - Mid-City

FALSTAFF BREWERY The Falstaff Brewery's iconic sign has towered over the Mid-City skyline since the early 20th Century. If the letters light up from top to bottom, the temperature is falling and vice versa. The weather ball changes to indicate weather conditions: green for fair, red for cloudy and flashing red and white for approaching storms. The statue on top of the old brewery is King Gambrinus, patron saint of beer drinkers and brewers, with his pet goat "Bock." **See: Dixie, Jax Brewery, Mid-City**

FAMILY GRAS is a family-friendly Carnival celebration that takes place in Metairie the weekend before Mardi Gras. The translation is literally: "Fat Family." It is my duty to point that out. **See: Mardi Gras**

FAST EDDIE is a loving reference to four-term governor of Louisiana, Edwin W. Edwards, who is forever ensconced in wax at Museé Conti for the veneration of future generations. **See: Conti**

FAT CITY is a section of Metairie anchored by Severn Avenue north of Veterans Memorial Boulevard. It is popular for its restaurants, bars and shops. **See: Metairie**

FAT TUESDAY See: Carnival, Mardi Gras

FAUBOURG (FOE berg), literally false town, is the French term for a suburb of the area defined by the original city. In our case, any neighborhood outside of the French Quarter. To make things interesting, there is a city north of Opelousas called Fouborge, a subdivision in New Orleans East spelled Fauberg and an alternative music celebration in Marigny known as Foburg Fest. No one said this would be easy. **See: Bouligny, Marigny, Tremé**

FILÉ (FEE lay) consists of dried sassafras leaves ground into a powder. This gift of the Choctaw Indians was originally used to thicken Gumbo when okra was not in season. Filé is added to Gumbo when it is served, not during cooking. **See: Gumbo**

FILMORE STREET passes through several Gentilly neighborhoods, including Filmore Gardens, and is often misspelled Fillmore. The city of Fillmore in Bossier Parish is spelled with the double L. **See: Vermilion**

FIVE ISLANDS refers to the five salt domes found in the coastal marshes of Louisiana. They include Avery Island, Belle Isle, Cote Blanche Island, Jefferson Island and Weeks Island **See: Avery Island, Cote Blanche Island**

FLAMBEAUX (flahm BO) Witnessing the spectacle of blazing torches is an unforgettable sight during Carnival. It is the traditional way to light up the elaborate floats during night parades. This time-honored custom is still carried out by African American men in white robes. It is customary to toss coins or hand money to them as they strut and dance along the parade route. **See: Mardi Gras**

[Fleur de Lis Dr street sign]

FLEUR-DE-LIS (FLURE de LEE) The fleur-de-lis is a stylized iris; literally translated from French as flower of the lily. It is a favorite symbol of the City of New Orleans as well as Baton Rouge, Acadiana and the New Orleans Saints. It is usually written with hyphens except on the street signs in Lakeview. Plural: fleurs-de-lis.

FLORIDA PARISHES A region of Louisiana consisting of eight parishes: East Baton Rouge, East and West Feliciana, Livingston, St. Helena, St. Tammany, Tangipihoa and Washington. These North Shore parishes were part of the Republic of West Florida and were not included in the original Louisiana Purchase. Interstate 12 which runs through the Florida Parishes is officially called the Republic of West Florida Parkway. **See: North Shore, River Parishes**

FLYING HORSES
Carousel Gardens - City Park

FLYING HORSES is a local reference for a carousel, specifically the historic 1906 carousel in City Park. A carousel 'flyer' is a horse that goes up and down as opposed to a 'stander.' The carousel features the work of famed carvers Looff, Carmel and Murphy.

FLYING HORSES
Post-Katrina Restoration - City Park
July 2006

FONTAINEBLEAU DRIVE (FON tan blow) The name is taken from the town in France. Local pronunciation can vary, (FOUN tan blue), depending on your neighborhood.

It also falls victim to a variety of spellings around town including this misspelled street sign. **See: Crossroads**

FORT MACOMB is a 19th century fortress on Chef Menteur Pass just south of Fort Pike. Note: The city in Mississippi is spelled McComb. **See: Chef Menteur, Lacombe, Spanish Fort**

FRENCH BREAD True New Orleans French bread is baked in old brick ovens producing a crunchy crust with an airy center resembling cotton candy. Similar to a baguette in France, it is the traditional bread for a New Orleans po-boy. Incidentally, the best French loaves in New Orleans are baked by German and Italian bakers. **See: Dressed, Pain Perdu, Po-Boy**

FRERET STREET (fruh RET) sometimes (fuh RET)
This Uptown street and neighborhood are named for William Freret.

Quaint Essential New Orleans

"WAITING UNDER THE CLOCK"
Ignatius J. Reilly - Canal Street - CBD

G IS FOR GRIS-GRIS

GALATOIRE'S (GAL uh twahs) is a venerable restaurant on Bourbon Street in the French Quarter. Galatoire's specializes in French Creole cooking. **See: Tujague's**

GALLERY An example of a cast iron gallery is on the Pontalba Apartments overlooking Jackson Square. Unlike a balcony, a gallery often runs around more than one side of a building and is usually covered. Some tourist brochures mistakenly refer to the Pontalba gallery as a wrought iron balcony. **See: Balcony, Cast Iron, Wrought Iron**

GALLIER STREET (GAL yer) This pronunciation is true for the street in Bywater as well as Gallier Hall; both named for the architect, James Gallier. Visitors tend to pronounce it (GAL yay). **See: Villere**

GAYOSO (guy O so) is a street in the New Orleans neighborhood of Mid-City. **See: Mid-City**

GENTILLY RIDGE is a stretch of high ground that runs along the former banks of Bayou Gentilly. Gentilly Road was built on the ridge and is part of the Old Spanish Trail that ran from Florida to California. One of the largest districts in New Orleans, Gentilly is comprised of twenty-two distinct neighborhoods, three universities, a seminary and of course, a rum distillery. **See: Broad, Crete, Indian Village, Milneburg, Pontilly**

GERMAN COAST is basically St. John the Baptist and St. Charles Parishes. Early German immigrants settled there to farm along the banks of the Mississippi River. **See: Des Allemands, River Parishes**

GERT TOWN Also known as Zion City, this Mid-City neighborhood is named for Alfred Gehrke. It is the location of Xavier University. Modern spelling is two words but it can still be seen in print and in web searches as Gerttown.
See: Crossroads, Mid-City, Xavier

GNO is an acronym for Greater New Orleans. The U.S. Census includes seven parishes as part of the New Orleans Metropolitan Area: Jefferson, Orleans, Plaquemines, St. Bernard, St. Tammany, St. Charles and St. John the Baptist.
See: SUNO, UNO

GO-CUP New Orleans is the only place I know where you can take your drink from one bar to another or drink as you walk on the streets of the French Quarter - as long as it is in a plastic cup. Just ask for a go-cup.

You know you are a New Orleanian when you are between bars when it is raining and you cover your cocktail instead of your head. **See: Hurricane**

GOVERNOR NICHOLLS This street, named for Gov. Francis T. Nicholls, begins in the French Quarter and is often misspelled with a single L as found in these street tiles.

It is never called Nicholls Street. **See: Douglass**

GO-ZONE Gulf Opportunity Zone refers to federal legislation that created a series of various tax incentives and programs to encourage investment in the areas devastated by Hurricanes Katrina and Rita. **See: LRA, RSD**

GRAMERCY (GRAM ur see) is a town in St. James Parish and home to Zapp's Potato Chips. **See: Zapp's**

GRAMERCY BRIDGE crosses the Mississippi River at Gramercy and connects St. James Parish with St. John the Baptist Parish. It is officially called The Veterans Memorial Bridge. **See: Claiborne Bridge, Green Bridge**

GRAND ISLE is an island and a town located at the southern tip of Jefferson Parish. Grand Isle hosts the annual Tarpon Rodeo in July. The island's history is tied to the privateer Jean Lafitte. Be careful not to refer to it as Grand Island. **See: Isles Dernières, Lafitte**

GRANDMA BEADS are lines of dirt and sweat around a child's neck after playing outside on the banquette all day. **See: Banquette, Bo Bo, Hickey**

GREASING OF THE POLES This Carnival tradition takes place on the Friday before Mardi Gras. Hotel and restaurant owners smear Vaseline on their gallery supports to deter tourists from climbing them to grab a pair of beads - or grab a pair of anything, for that matter. **See: Mardi Gras, Pair of Beads**

GREEN BRIDGE is the unofficial name for the Paris Road Bridge carrying Interstate 510 and Highway 47 across the Intracoastal Waterway. It connects St. Bernard Parish with New Orleans East. Although repainted in recent years, the name Green still applies. **See: da Parish, MRGO, Paris Road**

GRILLADES (GREE yods) are very thin and tender slices of beef or veal, browned and cooked in gravy and served with grits. Grillades and grits is a very traditional Creole brunch or breakfast dish. It is also traditionally served at debutante parties and the queen's midnight supper following a Carnival ball. **See: Ball, Creole, Pannéed Veal**

GRIP is vernacular for a small overnight bag or suitcase taken on a trip. **See: Locker**

GRIS-GRIS (GREE gree)   Usually written with a hyphen, gris-gris is a magical potion of various crushed herbs concealed in a small bag and used in the practice of Voodoo. **See: Voodoo, Wishing Spot**

GROSSE TETE (gros TATE) or (gros TET) is a village in Iberville Parish pronounced either way. It is French for big head. **See: Iberville**

GULF SOUTH refers to the region that includes Alabama, Mississippi and Louisiana. Strangely enough, the reference does not include Texas or Florida. **See: Bayou Country**

GUMBO Seafood gumbo is a roux-based stew with an essential ingredient being okra. The word gumbo comes from the African word for okra. Other variations such as filé gumbo and chicken or sausage gumbo do not always include okra.

The term has also become synonymous with any variety of local items mixed together, such as a gumbo of cultures or a musical gumbo. **See: Filé, Holy Trinity, Okra, Roux**

GUMBO YA YA is the quintessential gumbo served at Mr. B's in the French Quarter. *Gumbo Ya Ya* is also a WPA era book describing the culture and traditions of Louisiana. The reference means everybody talking all at once.

Quaint Essential New Orleans

GUMBO Z'HERBES (gumbo z'ehhb) is sometimes called greens gumbo or gumbo vert. This meatless version of gumbo, with an herb base, is traditionally made on Holy Thursday and served at Dooky Chase's. **See: Pointe Aux Herbes**

GREATLY EXAGGERATED
Fats Domino's House - Lower Nine
December 2005

H IS FOR HUBIG'S PIES

HAMMOND HIGHWAY once connected New Orleans to the city of Hammond. Only bits and pieces remain after it was replaced by Highway 51. One small length connects West End Boulevard in Lakeview with Chickasaw Avenue in Bucktown. The sign in Lakeview reads N.O. Hammond Highway. In Bucktown the signs read Metairie Hammond Highway.
See: Bucktown, Indian Beach, West End

HAYNE BOULEVARD (HAYN) in New Orleans East is named for Frank B. Hayne - not Haynes. There is no S at the end of his name. However, let's not tell that to the fine folks who run the Haynes Discount Market! There is a town called Haynesville in Claiborne Parish. **See: Little Woods**

HEAD OF PASSES is where the Mississippi River breaks off into three separate branches as it enters the Gulf of Mexico. The "head" is the actual mouth of the river and upriver mileages are measured from there. For example, Algiers is at mile 94.6 AHP (above Head of Passes). **See: Delta, Pilottown**

HENNESSY STREET This Mid-City street is named for former New Orleans Police Chief David Hennessy. The tiles in the banquette are correct; however the street signs are all misspelled.

In order to find this street with an internet map search, you have to misspell it: Hennessey! **See: Mid-City, Who Killa' Da Chief?**

HERBSAINT (HERB saint) This anise-flavored liqueur was originally made in New Orleans as a substitute for the outlawed absinthe in cocktails. It is an essential ingredient in an Herbsaint Frappé and a Sazerac. Herbsaint is an anagram for absinthe. **See: Peychaud's Bitters, Sazerac**

HICKEY A hickey is not a love bite in New Orleans. It is a knot or lump on one's head after you bump into something. **See: Passion Mark**

HIGH-RISE is a specific reference to the elevated portion of Interstate 10 as it crosses the Industrial Canal. The reference "high-rise bridge" is really unnecessary since we use the term exclusively for the bridge and not for tall buildings. **See: Industrial Canal**

HIGHWAY 11 BRIDGE is the common reference to the original concrete bridge crossing eastern Lake Pontchartrain and connecting Orleans and St. Tammany Parishes. Prior to the construction of Interstate 10, the Highway 11 bridge was known as the Pontchartrain Bridge or the five-mile Bridge. Its official name is the Robert Maestri Bridge and should not be confused with the Twin Spans. **See: Causeway, Maestri, Twin Spans**

HOG HEAD CHEESE is sometimes written "hogs head" cheese. This is a spicy local version of head cheese; basically meat suspended in gelatin. Tradition suggests that "fromage de tete" was made from everything that fell on the floor in the butcher shop. The recipe in the Picayune Creole Cook Book begins: "Remove eyes, ears and teeth from a hog's head. Place head and foot in boiling water ..." Well, you get the idea. **See: Cracklins**

HO JO MASSACRE If you were living in New Orleans on January 7, 1973; chances are you were glued to your TV set watching reporter Alec Gifford literally sweating bullets during the Howard Johnson Sniper Incident. The term, "Ho Jo Massacre," has become the official local reference to the two-day siege. **See: Rault Center**

HOLLYGROVE This neighborhood in the Carrollton district of New Orleans is written as one word. Musicians Johnny Adams and Theryl deClouet hail from Hollygrove.

HOLLYWOOD SOUTH is the official reference to the ever-expanding film industry in Louisiana, centered in New Orleans. **See: Broadway South**

HOLMES The quintessential meeting place for shoppers on Canal Street was under the clock at (HOLM zes) - the D. H. Holmes Department Store in the 800 block. There is a statue there of Ignatius J. Reilly waiting under the clock for his mother while, "... studying the crowd of people for signs of bad taste in dress." Unfortunately D. H. Holmes "Ain't Dere No More." **See: Ain't Dere No More**

HOLY TRINITY refers to a set of three ingredients essential to a particular style of cooking especially Creole and Cajun cuisine. The holy trinity includes celery, bell (or green) peppers and onions which are usually sautéed together.
See: Gumbo

HONEY ISLAND SWAMP MONSTER Honey Island Swamp is considered to be one of the most pristine swampland habitats in the United States. This swamp is also the home of the legendary Honey Island Swamp Monster, which has from time to time been known as the Tainted Keitre.
See: Atchafalaya

HORSE-DRAWN CARRIAGES I hate to be the one to tell you this. You know those picturesque horse-drawn carriages touring the French Quarter? Well, they're mule-drawn. You see, mules have better tolerance for the summer heat and the tourists really don't know the difference.

HOUMA (HOE muh) is a city in Terrebonne Parish also known for its Mardi Gras festivities. An offshoot of the Choctaw Indians settled in this area which the natives called Chukahoma, or 'red house.' You will also hear the city pronounced (WHO ma) by folks from the area. **See: Mardi Gras, Terrebonne**

HUBIG'S PIES (HYOO bigs) are fruit-filled fried pies made by "Savory Simon" Hubig resembling a turnover. Hubig's bakery opened in 1922 on Dauphine Street in Faubourg Marigny. On July 20, 2012, this New Orleans institution burned to the ground. Fortunately the owners have promised the city that they will restore, rebuild, and Re-Hubig. **See: Marigny**

HUCK-A-BUCK A 7th, 8th and 9th Ward reference for a frozen ice cup traditionally made with Kool-Aid in a Dixie cup. Known as a "freezie" in many neighborhoods. Just ask the Huck-A-Buck Lady. **See: Sno-Ball**

HURRICANE Pat O'Brien's in the French Quarter is famous for this cocktail made from passion fruit syrup and rum. It was created during World War II when whiskey was in short supply. The drink is served in a glass shaped like a hurricane lamp, thus the name. **See: Sazerac**

HURRICANE PARTY There was a time when extended families would all join together at one house to ride out a hurricane and watch Nash Roberts update the storm track with his famous black felt-tip pen. That was before Katrina. Today, extended families join together and run like the devil. **See: Katrina Tattoo**

HUSH PUPPY is a ball of deep fried cornmeal served alongside a variety of seafood dishes. Tradition suggests that the Ursuline Nuns, while cooking, would toss these morsels to barking dogs to quiet them. **See: Ursulines**

Quaint Essential New Orleans

THE FOUNTAIN OF THE WINDS
Enrique Alférez – Lakefront Airport

I IS FOR IRISH CHANNEL

IBERVILLE STREET (EYE ber vil) The street in the French Quarter and the parish are pronounced this way. However, the French pronunciation of Pierre Le Moyne d'Iberville is (Pe air Lay Moin Dye ber Veel). Iberville was the founder and governor of the first French colony of Louisiana. There are occasions when you might hear locals say (IB er vil), with a short i, when referring to the housing project or parish.
See: Bienville, Projects

ICE BOX You will still hear the term "ice box" in New Orleans. Refrigerator has way too many syllables.
See: Grip, Locker

INDIAN BEACH is a section of the lakefront in Metairie extending from Bucktown to the Causeway. **See: Coconut Beach, Bucktown**

Welcome To INDIAN VILLAGE

INDIAN VILLAGE is a small, isolated neighborhood in Gentilly just across Chef Menteur Highway from the Baptist Seminary with street names such as Pocahontas, Hiawatha, Powhatan and Iroquois. **See: Musicians' Village, Pines Village**

INDUSTRIAL CANAL is the common reference to the Inner Harbor Navigation Canal. It is a 5.5-mile canal connecting the Mississippi River to Lake Pontchartrain via a lock system. It bisects the Ninth Ward of New Orleans, separating the Upper and Lower Nine. **See: Claiborne Bridge, High-Rise, Ninth Ward**

INK PEN A ball-point or any type of pen in New Orleans.

INTERSTATE 10 When referring to Interstate 10 it is sufficient to just say "I-10." It isn't necessary to say: "the I-10," because you would not say: "the Interstate 10." *The*, is a definite article; *10*, is a definite interstate - get it? You don't need both! I feel much better now!
Parts of I-10 in Louisiana are named. The stretch between Lafayette and Baton Rouge is the Atchafalaya Swamp Freeway. The section between the 610 split in Lakeview to Claiborne Avenue is called the Pontchartrain Expressway. The final stretch from Slidell to Mississippi is called the Stephen Ambrose Memorial Highway. **See: Atchafalaya, CCC, High-Rise, Toni Morrison Interchange**

INTRACOASTAL WATERWAY is a toll-free waterway that runs from New Jersey to Brownsville, Texas. It traverses the wetlands of Louisiana and is sometimes misrepresented as the Intercoastal Waterway. There is a town in Louisiana called Intracoastal City. **See: Green Bridge, Industrial Canal, Seabrook**

IRISH BAYOU, Irish Bayou Lagoon and the Irish Bayou Canal are located in extreme eastern New Orleans near the intersection of I-10 and Highway 11. Actually the entire triangular area called South Point is more commonly referred to as Irish Bayou. **See: Little Woods, Pointe aux Herbes**

IRISH CHANNEL is not a waterway and should not be confused with Irish Bayou or a cable TV network.
It is an historic neighborhood located in the Uptown area near the Mississippi River. Its borders are basically Magazine Street, the river, First and Toledano Streets. It was originally settled by Irish immigrants in the early 19th century and is ground zero for St. Patrick's Day celebrations and parades.
See: St. Patrick's Day

ISLEÑOS (is LAYN yos)   Descendants of Canary Islanders came to America and settled in St. Bernard Parish where most of the traditional Los Isleños (The Islanders) customs continue to this day. Isleños communities include: Delacroix Island, Reggio, Yscloskey, Shell Beach and Hopedale. They are sometimes referred to as Spanish Cajuns. **See: Cajun, Delacroix, Yscloskey**

ISLES DERNIÈRES (EEL dern YARE)   Last Islands, originally called Isle Dernière, is a barrier island on the Louisiana coast. It was devastated by the hurricane of 1856. The hotel and surrounding establishments were destroyed, over 200 people perished and the island was split in half. It is now referred to in the plural. It is a haven for pelicans and other seabirds. **See: Grand Isle**

ITALIAN PLAZA is officially known as Piazza d'Italia and located at Lafayette and Commerce Streets just off of Poydras Street. It is known as the city's secluded masterpiece of post-modern architecture. **See: Spanish Plaza**

ITALIAN QUARTER   In the early 19th century, part of the French Quarter between Chartres and Decatur streets and from Barracks to Dumaine was sometimes referred to as Little Palermo. **See: Muffuletta**

J IS FOR JAMBALAYA

JACKSON BARRACKS This military reservation used by the National Guard marks the eastern boundary of New Orleans in the lower Ninth Ward. This is not to be confused with Jackson Square. **See: Ninth Ward**

FRENCH QUARTER FESTIVAL
Jackson Square - April 2007

JACKSON SQUARE Named for Battle of New Orleans hero Andrew Jackson, this historic park is the centerpiece of the French Quarter. Originally called the Place d'Armes. It was designed in a solar pattern in honor of Louis XIV, the "Sun King." **See: Place d'Armes, Vieux Carré**

JAHNCKE (JANG kee) Road is located in New Orleans East and is named for Fritz Jahncke who is responsible for much of the development along the New Orleans lakefront.

JAMBALAYA (jam buh LIE uh) is made in one pot with chicken and/or sausage, vegetables and rice. Creole jambalaya is sometimes called jambalaya rouge, whereas Cajun jambalaya blanc usually contains no tomatoes. The Picayune's Creole Cook Book calls it a Creole Spanish dish. Gonzales, Louisiana, is the Jambalaya Capital of the World.
See: Cajun, Creole, Gumbo

COUSIN'S BEER PARLOR
North Rampart Street - Bywater
August 1985

JAX BREWERY Jax is the official moniker for the Jackson Brewing Company across from the upper Pontalba Building in the French Quarter. Jax Beer was once brewed there. It has been converted into restaurants and retail space.
See: Falstaff Brewery

JAZZ FEST The New Orleans Jazz & Heritage Festival, commonly called the Jazz Fest, is an annual celebration of the music and culture of New Orleans and Louisiana held at the Fair Grounds. The festival originated in Congo Square in 1970.
See: Chaz Fest, Congo Square, Fair Grounds

BLACK FEATHER BIG CHIEF LIONEL DELPIT
Jazz Funeral - St. Roch - July 2011

JAZZ FUNERAL This honorary funeral procession through the streets of New Orleans is traditionally reserved for deceased musicians. A grand marshal leads fellow musicians and marchers with a dirge. Following the burial, the music becomes more joyful and spirited. A second line generally follows with umbrellas and waving handkerchiefs.

When someone dies in New Orleans you book a marching brass band – and then you call the coroner. **See: Second Line, Social Aid and Pleasure Club**

JEAN LAFITTE (ZHAN lah FEET) or (GENE lah FEET) This town in Jefferson Parish is named for everyone's favorite local privateer and smuggler. There is also the small village of Lafitte nearby. **See: Lafitte, Pirates Alley**

JEFFERSON DAVIS PARISH, in the Acadiana region of southwest Louisiana, is named for the President of the Confederacy. Do not confuse this with Jefferson Parish in southeast Louisiana which was named after Thomas Jefferson. **See: Acadiana**

Also, Jefferson Davis Memorial Parkway in New Orleans is known as monument row for the collection of Civil War memorials in Mid-City. Both, the parish and parkway are simply referred to as Jeff Davis. Do not confuse this with Jefferson Highway in Jefferson Parish. **See: Mid-City**

JOURDAN Named for Raoul Jourdan, this street runs along the eastern length of the Industrial Canal and is often misspelled Jordan. The family pronunciation is (Zhor DAHN) but that's a little too proper for locals. **See: Industrial Canal**

K IS FOR KING CAKE

K&B PURPLE refers to a distinct shade of purple used in the logo of the former K&B Drug Stores. You still hear locals refer to that specific color as K&B purple. **See: Ain't Dere No More**

KATRINA FATIGUE A generalized indifference to the Katrina disaster manifested by malaise, exhaustion, despair, anger and impatience directed towards the government, media coverage and even attempts to remember or memorialize the event. **See: K-Ville**

KATRINA TATTOO refers to those ubiquitous slash marks that search parties spray-painted on our houses after Hurricane Katrina that we are still trying to remove. **See: Blue Roof**

KEEPER If you catch a crab at the Lake Pontchartrain seawall and it is heavy and at least five inches across...it's a keeper. **See: Crab Trap, Loaded She, Seawall**

KENNER BEND refers to the bend in the Mississippi River just south of the Louis Armstrong Airport. **See: Algiers Point**

KERLEREC (KEL a wreck)   This Marigny street is named for French Governor, Louis B. de Kerlerec. The first R is not pronounced. **See: Marigny**

KING CAKE is inseparable from the Carnival season which begins on Twelfth Night.   January 6th is also known as the Epiphany and Le Petit Noel. The oval cake is made of braided dough topped with icing and sprinkled with purple, green and gold sugar granules.   It contains a hidden plastic baby. If you eat the piece of cake with the baby, you provide the king cake for the next party unless, of course, you choke to death.   Some local bakeries now sell king cakes year round which is an egregious break with tradition.   **See: Carnival, Krewe, Phunny Phorty Phellows, Twelfth Night**

KISATCHIE (kis SAT chee)   The only national forest in Louisiana is located in the piney hills of seven central and northern parishes. It is Choctaw for reed or cane break river. Not to be confused with the town of Keatchie (KEE-chee) in DeSoto Parish.

KREWE (CREW) The Mistick Krewe of Comus is historically credited with the origin and spelling of this term. A krewe is a private Carnival organization that puts on a parade and/or a ball in New Orleans. All expenses for the krewe's activities, including the parade, are financed by krewe members. Traditionally, there is no commercial sponsorship of Carnival activities. **See: Mardi Gras, Mistick Krewe of Comus, Throw**

Quaint Essential New Orleans

KREWE FAVOR is a souvenir gift that a krewe member gives to a dance partner or "call-out" at a Carnival ball.
See: Ball, Call-Out, Mardi Gras

K-VILLE Short for Katrinaville, this 2007 cable TV cop show depicted life in New Orleans after Hurricane Katrina. It was fairly well-received except for the curiously ill-conceived concept of "Gumbo Parties" which became a local joke.
See: Hurricane Party, Katrina Fatigue

KATRINA ANGEL
St. Roch Cemetery - St. Roch

L IS FOR LAGNIAPPE

LABORDE LOOKOUT This artificial mountain can be found hidden within the Couturie Forest and Arboretum in City Park. It was named for former park manager, Ellis Laborde. Built from riprap during the construction of I-610, it is reported to be the highest spot in New Orleans at 27.5 feet. Monkey Hill in Audubon Park is 25.4 feet. It is now simply referred to as "the Mountain" in City Park. **See: Couturie, Monkey Hill**

LACOMBE (la KOME) is a city in St. Tammany Parish, often misspelled LaComb. It was the home of Louisiana's famed Chahta Ima, missionary to the Choctaw Indians. **See: Fort Macomb**

LAFAYETTE SQUARE (LAH fay YET) Located in the CBD, this park was the American Sector's version of Jackson Square. The square contains statues of John McDonogh, Henry Clay and Benjamin Franklin; but alas, none for the Marquis de La Fayette. **See: CBD, McDonogh**

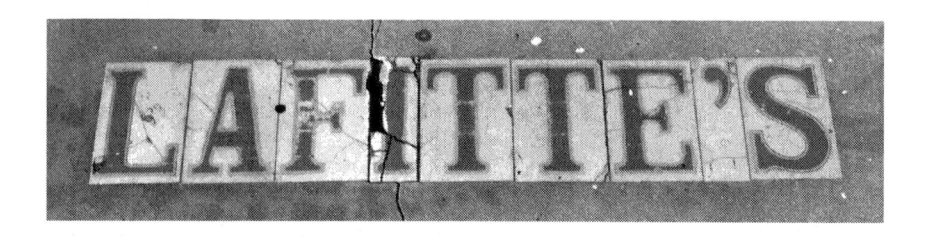

LAFITTE (la FEET) is a village in Jefferson Parish named for privateer Jean Lafitte. Just north of Lafitte is a Cajun fishing village called Jean Lafitte. Both are located on Bayou Barataria. An interesting footnote is that brothers Jean and Pierre signed their names on official documents with two Fs: *Laffite*. **See: Jean Lafitte**

LAFITTE PROJECTS was a housing project in the Tremé-Lafitte neighborhood, razed after Katrina to make way for a new mixed income development called Faubourg Lafitte. **See: Projects**

LAFOURCHE (la FOOSH) is a parish and bayou in southeast Louisiana. **See: Grand Isle**

LAFRENIERE PARK (LA fren YERE) is the largest park in Metairie. This park and a street in New Orleans were named for Nicolas Chauvin de la Freniere.

LAGNIAPPE (LAHN yap) Means a little something extra. A small gift given to a customer by a merchant at the time of a purchase; like a 13th McKenzie's buttermilk drop when you order a dozen. **See: Make Groceries**

LAISSEZ LES BONS TEMPS ROULER (lay zay lay BOHN TOHN rew lay) is the unofficial motto of Cajun Country and most of Louisiana for that matter: "Let the good times roll!" I have never heard another human being utter this phrase in my entire life. It only appears on tourist brochures and t-shirts. **See: Louisiana**

LAKE BORGNE (BORN) Due to the loss of wetlands, Lake Borgne is really a saltwater bay or lagoon. The name comes from the French word meaning one-eyed. Remember the silent G.

LAKE CATHERINE The official name of this lake in eastern New Orleans is Lake St. Catherine. It is a small brackish-water lake between Lakes Pontchartrain and Borgne. The general area is referred to as the Lake Catherine neighborhood. It is well-known for its cleverly named fishing camps that line Highway 90 from Chef Pass to the Rigolets. **See: Chef Menteur, Little Woods, Rigolets**

LAKEFRONT ARENA This is the common reference for the Nat G. Kiefer UNO Lakefront Arena located on the east campus on Franklin Avenue. **See: Norena, UNO**

LAKESHORE Lakeshore and lakefront are written as one word as are the neighborhoods of Lakeview, Lakewood and Laketown. However, Lake Vista, Lake Terrace and Lake Oaks are two words. **See: South Shore**

LAPALCO (la PAL ko) This boulevard that runs through West Jefferson is an acronym for the Louisiana Power and Light Company. **See: Norco**

LAPEYROUSE STREET (LA pay rewz) This street named for John Lapeyrouse runs through the Seventh Ward.

LAPLACE (la PLAHS) is a city in St. John the Baptist Parish. Alternate spellings of La Place and Laplace appear to be acceptable considering their prevalence on maps and in print. However, it should never be pronounced like the word 'place.' LaPlace is the host city for the annual Andouille Festival. **See: Andouille, German Coast**

LAST ISLAND   See: Isles Dernières

LEAKE AVENUE is a section of River Road that runs from Audubon Park through Riverbend. The Corps of Engineers, the agency responsible for our hurricane protection levees, has its headquarters on Leake Avenue. Does this surprise anyone?

LEEVILLE is a village in southern Lafourche Parish closely associated with the oil industry and shrimp processing – and we know how well those two go together.
See: Leesville, Lafourche

LEESVILLE is a city in Vernon Parish known for its proximity to the Fort Polk Military Reservation.

LEONIDAS (lee YANH uh dus) Named for Leonidas K. Polk; this is the official name of the Uptown neighborhood centered on the intersection of Leonidas Street and S. Claiborne Avenue. Pronounced by neighbors as (lee YON dis). Many old-timers still refer to the upper section of Leonidas as West Carrollton. Southwest of the intersection of S. Carrollton and S. Claiborne Avenues is known as Pigeon Town.
See: Black Pearl, Carrollton, Pension Town

LINCOLN BEACH was an African American amusement park on the lakefront in Little Woods that operated from 1939-1965 during segregation. The area along the lake is now used for fishing and swimming and is still called Lincoln Beach.
See: Coconut Beach, Little Woods, Pontchartrain

LITTLE SAIGON is a local reference to the vibrant Vietnamese community centered along Alcee Fortier Boulevard in New Orleans East. **See: Versailles, Village de l'Est**

LITTLE WOODS This large area of New Orleans East between Lake Pontchartrain and Interstate 10 is officially called Little Woods/Edgelake. Little Woods traditionally referred to the area surrounding the intersection of Hayne Boulevard and Paris Road. It was called the poor man's Miami Beach for the fishing camps that once lined the shore for miles until Hurricanes Gustav and Katrina wiped them out. Many of the camps were second homes for vacationing New Orleanians. **See: Hayne Boulevard, Lincoln Beach**

LITTLE PALERMO was actually a section of the French Quarter so named for its mostly Sicilian population.
See: Italian Plaza, Italian Quarter

LIZARD What we commonly refer to as a lizard in New Orleans is really called a green anole or Carolina anole elsewhere. Although it changes colors, is it not a true chameleon. **See: Locust**

LIZARDI STREET (li ZAR dee) This street, named for a prominent New Orleans family, runs through the Lower Ninth Ward. Some of the street tiles are misspelled.
See: Ninth Ward

LOADED SHE is a local reference for a sponge crab; a female crab carrying eggs or roe. The condition is obvious by the orange protrusion from the abdominal apron. If caught in a trap or net, they should always be carefully returned to the water. Other references are busted sook and berried crab.
See: Crab Trap, Soft Shell Crab

LOCKER is the New Orleans word for a closet. It is believed that closets were taxed as rooms in New Orleans so people used lockers or armoires for clothing storage. With the return of closets in home construction, the term locker stuck.
See: Grip

LOCUST What we refer to as a locust in New Orleans is really a cicada. A true locust is a form of grasshopper.
See: Lizard, Mosquito Hawk

LOOP is the acronym for the Louisiana Offshore Oil Port near Port Fourchon which is used for offloading and storing crude oil from some of the largest tankers in the world. Not to be confused with the Gulf of Mexico loop current.
See: Port Fourchon

LOUISIANA (luh WEE zee AN nuh) The French explorer, René Robert Cavelier, Sieur de La Salle, named Louisiana for Louis XIV, King of France. In some parts of the state, as well as some song lyrics, you might hear people pronounce it (LEW zee an nuh), however, please don't do that in public!

LOUISIANAN / LOUISIANIAN Pertaining to Louisiana or someone from Louisiana. **See: New Orleanian**

LOUISIANA STATE SEAL The State Seal depicts a mother Brown Pelican, the State Bird, in the act of vulning. She is surrounded by three chicks and is shown tearing at her flesh in order to feed her young. In reality, Louisiana politicians tear at each other's flesh and eat their young. The State motto "Union, Justice, Confidence" surrounds the birds. On the state seal and flag, the brown pelican is white.
See: New Orleans City Seal

LRA is an acronym for the Louisiana Recovery Authority. It is a state planning entity created to assist in the rebuilding process in response to Hurricane Katrina. **See: CDBG, RSD**

LUCKY BEANS are the dried fava beans found on all St. Joseph's altars in New Orleans. During the Sicilian famine, the fava bean is said to have thrived when other crops failed. **See: St. Joseph's Day**

LUCKY DOGS are hot dogs that are sold from seven-foot-long wiener-shaped carts. They have operated on the street corners of New Orleans since 1947. **See: Roman Candy Man**

LULING BRIDGE in St. Charles Parish carries Interstate 310 across the Mississippi River connecting Highway 18 on the West Bank with Highway 48 on the East Bank. It is officially called the Hale Boggs Memorial Bridge.

LUNDI GRAS   The day before Mardi Gras is Lundi Gras or Fat Monday. Royalty from Zulu and Rex arrive by boat and meet near the foot of Canal Street at Spanish Plaza. It is also the day that the identities of Rex and his debutante queen are revealed to the public. The tradition of Lundi Gras began in 1874 but fell to the wayside until it was revived in 1987.
See: Mardi Gras, Rex, Spanish Plaza, Zulu

LYONS STREET (LIONS)   This Uptown street is named for the City of Lyon (lee YOHN) in France which was once spelled Lyons. However, in New Orleans, it's just plain (LIONS) street. **See: Cadiz, Milan**

THE CORPSES OF ENGINEERS
Seventeenth Street Canal Floodwall
December 2005 - Lakeview

CHAPEL AND SHRINE OF ST. ROCH
Campo Santo – Faubourg St. Roch
July 2006

M IS FOR MARDI GRAS

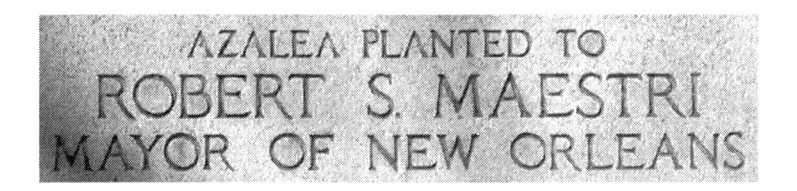

AZALEA PLANTED TO ROBERT S. MAESTRI MAYOR OF NEW ORLEANS

MAESTRI STREET (MAY stree) North and South Maestri, two streets that border Lafayette Square, are named for former Mayor Robert Maestri. Maestri was mayor from 1936-46. **See: Highway 11 Bridge, Lafayette Square**

MAGNOLIA PROJECTS was a Central City housing project renamed C. J. Peete and demolished after Katrina to make room for a mixed income development called Harmony Oaks. **See: Projects**

MAKE GROCERIES is a local expression meaning to go to the grocery. "I'm going to Schwegmann's to make groceries!" The term originated with the French-speaking Creoles who used the verb "faire," which means "to make" or "to do." **See: Lagniappe, Schwegmann's Bag**

MAMOU (mah MOO) This town in Evangeline Parish bills itself as the Cajun Music Capital of the World. Every year the town holds the Courir de Mardi Gras. 'Pass a good time' at Fred's Lounge. **See: Courir de Mardi Gras**

MANCHAC (MAN shack) Pass Manchac, once known as the Iberville River, is a waterway that connects Lakes Pontchartrain and Maurepas. There is a small town called Manchac just north of the pass. This spit of land is traversed by Highway 51 and Interstate 55. The entire area is referred to as Manchac. It is Choctaw for rear entrance. If you're headed to Manchac, it is probably for fried catfish at Middendorf's. It is said that the catfish is so thin it has only one side.
See: Maurepas, Pontchartrain

MARAIS STREET (muh RAY) This street that runs through Faubourg Tremé is French for marsh or swamp.
See: Faubourg, Perdido, Tremé

MARDI GRAS (MAR dee graw) is one day only and it means Fat Tuesday, the day of feasting. It is also known as Shrove Tuesday which is the day before Ash Wednesday. The reference Mardi Gras Day is redundant. The reference "the Mardi Gras" is unnecessary.

It is the ultimate day of the Carnival season, sometimes called Carnival Day, and falls forty-seven days before Easter. Some news organizations and tourists incorrectly refer to the entire Carnival season as the Mardi Gras season. Most of us reach high school before we learn that Mardi Gras is not a national holiday. Incidentally, it is Pancake Day in England – poor souls. **See: Carnival, Family Gras, Lundi Gras, Mistick Krewe of Comus, Rex, Zulu**

MARDI GRAS INDIANS Members of these traditional African American neighborhood tribes, dress in hand-made Native American costumes famous for elaborate bead and feather work. They generally appear on the streets of New Orleans on Mardi Gras, Super Sunday and at the Jazz Fest. They are also associated with St. Joseph's night. The group hierarchy is complex, including First Queen, spy boy, flag boy, and medicine man, but always led by the Big Chief.
See: Big Chief, St. Joseph's Day, Super Sunday

MARIE LAVEAU (la VOE) was the most influential Voodoo priestess of New Orleans. She was known as the Voodoo Queen. The family tomb is located in St. Louis Cemetery #1. Placing three Xs on her tomb is a meaningless custom and it is actually illegal to deface an historic monument. **See: Gris-Gris, Voodoo, Wishing Spot**

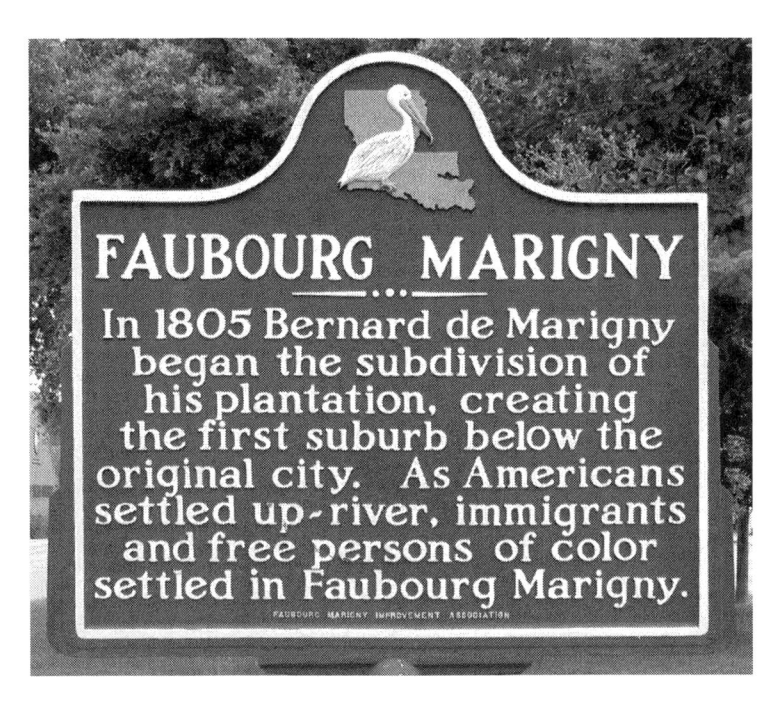

> **FAUBOURG MARIGNY**
>
> In 1805 Bernard de Marigny began the subdivision of his plantation, creating the first suburb below the original city. As Americans settled up-river, immigrants and free persons of color settled in Faubourg Marigny.

MARIGNY (MAH ruh nee) Faubourg Marigny is a suburb of the original city - the French Quarter. It is often referred to as "The Marigny." The neighborhood and street were named for Bernard Xavier Philippe de Marigny de Mandeville. After gambling away all of his money, his plantation was subdivided. One particular section between Elysian Fields and the French Quarter is called the Marigny Triangle. **See: Bouligny, Faubourg**

MARINGOUIN (MER in gwin) is a town in Iberville Parish that means swamp mosquito. Iberville wrote of the pesky 'maringouins' that kept his men awake at nights in the swamps of Louisiana. **See: Iberville**

MARRAINE (ma RAHN) refers to one's godmother in New Orleans and south Louisiana. The term Nainaine (na NAN) is also heard. **See: Parraine**

MARRERO (muh REH roe) is a city on the West Bank in Jefferson Parish which is often misspelled Marerro, or worse, Marrerro. **See: West Bank**

MARSHAL FOCH STREET (FOESH) This Lakeview street is named for Ferdinand Foch who became Marshal of France in 1918.

His first name was not Marshall, as it appears on some street signs.

MAUREPAS (MAHR a pah) Lake Maurepas is a brackish water lake connected to Lake Pontchartrain via Pass Manchac. The lake is named for Jean-Frédéric Phélypeaux, comte de Maurepas. **See: Manchac, Pontchartrain**

MAZANT STREET (MAY zant) in the Upper Ninth Ward of New Orleans begins in Bywater. **See: Bywater, Moisant, Ninth Ward**

McDONOGH John McDonogh was an eccentric entrepreneur and philanthropist famous for his endowments to public schools in New Orleans and Baltimore. McDonogh Day is the first Friday in May when school children traditionally place flowers by McDonogh's statue.

> Cabildo Building in N. O. in
> Acquired from Allard in 18
> J. McDonough -- given to N. O.

His name is often misspelled with a U, as illustrated by this historic plaque in City Park. Fortunately the public schools bear his name correctly. There is a section of Algiers called McDonoghville. **See: Bermuda Triangle**

MEETING OF THE COURTS The formal end of the Carnival season arrives with the ceremonial Meeting of the Courts on the evening of Mardi Gras. Although Rex is the King of Carnival, he and his queen are invited to visit with Comus and his consort at the conclusion of their masked ball. Rex and Comus escort each other's queen in the Grand March. **See: Ash Wednesday, Mistick Krewe of Comus, Municipal Auditorium, Rex**

MELPOMENE STREET (MEL puh meen)   The Greek Muse of Tragedy gets her own special pronunciation for her New Orleans street. **See: Calliope, Clio, Euterpe, Terpsichore**

MELTS refers to the lining of a cow's stomach used to bait crawfish nets. It is bloody, spongy, smelly and crawfish can't resist it. After unloading your catch, you step on the melt to make it ooze, and you toss the net back in the water. Yum!
See: Crawfish, Don't Eat The Dead Ones

MERAUX (MEER row)   A city in St. Bernard Parish often misspelled Mereaux. **See: Miro**

MER ROUGE   A village in Morehouse Parish which is French for Red Sea. **See: Baton Rouge**

METAIRIE (MET uh ree) is an unincorporated Jefferson Parish suburb of New Orleans. Metairie is a French term for the "little farms" tended by sharecroppers that developed from larger plantations. Old Metairie is the original part of the city centered along Metairie Road which follows the natural ridge formed by Bayou Metairie. There is a taxi company called Metry Cab (MET tree) since that is the way many locals pronounce it. It is often mispronounced in the media as (ma TARE ee). **See: Fat City, MSY**

MICHOUD (MEE shoo)   Named for Antoine Michoud, the boulevard and the general area in eastern New Orleans is the home of NASA's Michoud Assembly Facility. This former sugar plantation was the assembly site for the space shuttle's external fuel tanks. The official name for the neighborhood is Village de l'Est and is home to a vibrant Vietnamese community. The Vietnamese refer to the area as Versailles.
See: Little Saigon, Versailles, Village de l'Est

MID-CITY This large New Orleans neighborhood is officially written with a hyphen. There is a Carnival krewe call the Krewe of Mid-City. **See: Battle of the Bands**

MILAN STREET (MY lan) The New Orleans street and neighborhood, named for the city in Italy, bear a distinctly local pronunciation. **See: Cadiz, Lyons**

MILE HIGH PIE The Pontchartrain Hotel's signature dessert includes layers of various ice cream flavors, meringue and chocolate syrup. **See: Bananas Foster, Beignet**

MILNE (MIL nee) is a boulevard in the neighborhood of Lakeview which is often mispronounced (MILN). The old Milne Boys' Home is on Franklin Avenue near the neighborhood of Milneburg.

MILNEBURG (MIL nee berg) The area along the lakefront at the end of Elysian Fields was called Milneburg for former resident and businessman, Alexander Milne. Once called Old Lake End, it was a resort area important in the early history of jazz. Milneburg eventually became the site of the Pontchartrain Beach Amusement Park.

It was historically mispronounced Milenburg (MIL en berg) resulting in a famous jazz tune titled, *Milenburg Joys*.

Milneburg is now an official neighborhood anchored along St. Roch Avenue just north of Gentilly Terrace.

See: Gentilly Ridge, Pontchartrain Beach, West End

MILNEBURG LIGHTHOUSE
Elysian Fields Terminus - Lakefront

MIRABEAU STREET (MEER a boo)   This street, named for the Comte de Mirabeau, runs through the Gentilly District. Some locals pronounce it (MEER a boe) ... but don't do that. **See: De Saix, Fontainebleau**

MIRLITON (MEL a tahn) There is only one way to pronounce this vegetable in New Orleans, so start practicing. It is known in other parts as a chayote or vegetable pear. This member of the gourd family is often cooked and stuffed with shrimp. The annual Mirliton Festival is in Bywater's Markey Park where you can find mirlitons stuffed, fried and even pickled. **See: Alligator Pear, Bywater**

MIRO STREET (MEER row)   This street that runs across town is named for Spanish Governor Esteban Rodriguez Miró y Sabater. **See: Meraux**

Quaint Essential New Orleans

MR. BINGLE
"Jingle, jangle, jingle, here comes Mr. Bingle."
Mr. Bingle is a pop-culture icon of New Orleans; mascot of the former Maison Blanche Department Store on Canal Street. The Christmas display once included a live marionette show starring this little snowman assistant to Santa Claus. The large papier-mâché version can still be seen in the City Park Botanical Garden during the annual Celebration in the Oaks.
See: Celebration in the Oaks, Morgus

MR. BINGLE
Celebration in the Oaks – City Park
December 2006

Quaint Essential New Orleans

MISTICK KREWE OF COMUS (KO mus)   Known as the Mistick Krewe, (note the archaic spelling of Mystic), this is the oldest Carnival krewe in New Orleans (1857). In place of the traditional scepter, Comus carries a jeweled cup. There is no King of Comus, he is simply Comus; the god of festivity, revelry and nocturnal dalliances. There is also a women's Carnival organization known as the Mystic Club.
See: Krewe, Meeting of the Courts, Rex

MOISANT (MOY zant)   In 1910, daredevil aviator John Moisant crashed his plane in Kenner so they named an international airport for him. That's exactly what I would have done. In 2001 the name was changed to Louis Armstrong New Orleans International Airport. The airport is owned by the city of New Orleans but is located in Kenner.   **See: MSY**

MOM-N-EM   This term is generally associated with "Yat Speak" and refers to one's immediate family. It is actually used by most New Orleanians I know. "I'm goin' *by* my mom-n-em this year for Christmas."   **See: Yat**

MONKEY HILL at the Audubon Zoo was known as the highest point in New Orleans when we were kids. It was built by the WPA to give children an idea of what a real hill looked like. It is difficult to recognize today, having received the Audubon Institute's kitschy treatment including a tree house, rope bridges and lion sculptures. LIDAR imagery taken in 2007 measured the elevation of Monkey Hill at 25.4 feet. Alas, it is now dwarfed by Laborde Lookout in City Park's Couturie Forest which is 27.5 feet above sea level.   **See: Couturie Forest, Laborde Lookout**

MONKEY WRENCH CORNER   The riverside corner of Royal and Canal Streets in New Orleans is where unemployed sailors would try to beg or borrow money from one another.
See: Dead Man's Curve

Quaint Essential New Orleans

MOONWALK
NAMED IN HONOR OF
MOON LANDRIEU
In recognition of his leadership and vision

MOONWALK This linear park along the Mississippi River, across from Jackson Square, is named in honor of former Mayor Maurice "Moon" Landrieu. It should be written as one word. **See: Dutch Alley, Jackson Square, Riverwalk**

MORGANZA (mor GAN zuh) is a town in Pointe Coupee Parish and the location of a spillway that can divert Mississippi floodwaters into the Atchafalaya Basin.
See: Atchafalaya, Bonnet Carré, Pointe Coupee

MORGUSOTRONIC BILLBOARD
Loyola Avenue - CBD
Summer 2006

MORGUS (MOR gus)   Dr. Momus Alexander Morgus, aka Morgus the Magnificent, is the chief scientist in New Orleans. He is the founder of the Momus Alexander Morgus Institute or M.A.M.I. (Mammy), located over the old city ice house. Because his institute was non-profit, literally, he was forced to host bad sci-fi and horror movies on late-night TV between experiments beginning in the late 1950s. Nevertheless, he is a New Orleans icon of the Higher Order. **See: Mr. Bingle**

MORTUARY CHAPEL This is the common reference to what is now known as Our Lady of Guadalupe Chapel on N. Rampart Street in New Orleans. It was the burial church for victims of yellow fever due to its proximity to St. Louis Cemetery #1. **See: Yellow Jack**

MOSQUITO HAWK is the New Orleans reference for a dragonfly. **See: Locust**

MOUND AVENUE UNDERPASS The Pontchartrain Expressway, a section of I-10, forms an underpass where it intersects with the railroad trestle just south of the I-610 split in Lakeview. It is referred to as the Mound Avenue Railroad Underpass due to its proximity to that street. It is predictably misspelled Mounds or Moundes. **See: High-Rise**

MRGO (Mister Go) is an acronym for the Mississippi River-Gulf Outlet Canal, also written MR-GO. This 66-mile man-made channel cuts through St. Bernard Parish and provides a shortcut to New Orleans from the Gulf of Mexico. When MRGO was built, the channel was 650 feet wide. The average width is now 1,500 feet due to the loss of wetlands. This proved to be disastrous during Hurricane Katrina and the outlet is now closed. **See: da Parish**

MSY The abbreviation MSY on your luggage tag stands for Moisant Stock Yards, the airport code for Louis Armstrong New Orleans International Airport. The official airport website, www.flymsy.com, looks awfully close to the word flimsy - does this bother anyone else? **See: Moisant**

Quaint Essential New Orleans

"OOH POO PAH DOO"
Jessie Hill Grave - Holt Cemetery
August 2004

Quaint Essential New Orleans

MUSICIANS' VILLAGE is a post-Katrina cultural initiative created to replace flood damaged housing in a section of the Upper Ninth Ward. The village covers an area bounded by North Roman, Alvar and North Johnson Streets, including a section of Bartholomew Street. **See: Indian Village, Pines Village**

MUFFULETTA (muf a LET ta) This famous New Orleans Italian sandwich was invented at the Central Grocery in the French Quarter. It consists of a variety of Italian meats and cheeses topped with Italian salad and served on an Italian bun. It's an offer you can't refuse. **See: Little Palermo**

As you can see from the photo, spelling varies around town. There is also an alternate pronunciation: (moo foo LET ta). **See: Italian Quarter, Wop Salad**

MUNICIPAL AUDITORIUM This 1930s era facility in the Tremé neighborhood is best known as the traditional home for Carnival balls. Its official name is the Morris F. X. Jeff Sr. Municipal Auditorium. **See: Congo Square, Court, Tremé**

MYNEZ (MY nez) "Yat Speak" is an exaggeration of the way we talk. This pronunciation of mayonnaise, however, is actually heard around New Orleans. **See: Dressed, Mom-n-em, Yat**

N IS FOR NEUTRAL GROUND

NAPOLEON HOUSE
Chartres Street - French Quarter
April 2005

NAPOLEON Whatever the reference - Napoleon Avenue, Napoleon House or Napoleonville - please refrain from this common error: Napolean.

NATCHITOCHES (NAK uh dish) The Caddo word for chestnut eaters is the name of a city and parish in Central Louisiana. When local media types try to spell or pronounce this word, things can go horribly wrong. The Natchitoches meat pie is the official meat pie of the State of Louisiana in the event someone asks you. **See: Central Louisiana**

N'AWLINS is an exaggerated pronunciation of New Orleans attributed to "Yat Speak" but is rarely ever used except in song, local theatre productions or *Vic & Nat'ly* cartoons.

There is one notable exception: The popular N'Awlins Air Show held at the Naval Air Station-Joint Reserve Base in Belle Chasse. Apparently, they never did get the memo.
See: Belle Chasse, Mynez, Ninth Ward, Yat

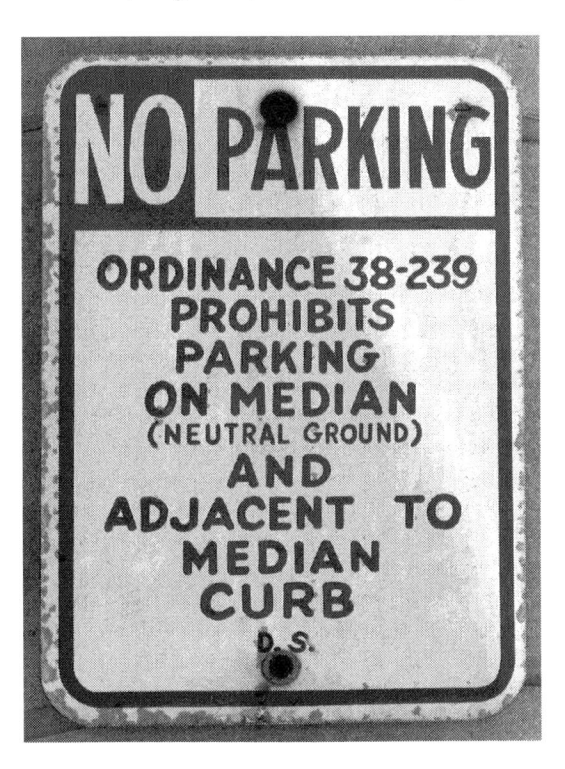

NEUTRAL GROUND Every median or traffic island along a New Orleans street is called a neutral ground. In the early days of New Orleans, Canal Street was the dividing line between the Creole French Quarter and the Americans residing Uptown. This strip of land was called the neutral ground thus setting the term for all medians in the city to this day. Parade riders will tell you to look for them on the neutral ground side or banquette side of their float. If you suddenly see cars illegally parked on the neutral ground; it's about to rain cats and dogs! **See: Banquette, Canal Street**

NEW OILEANS A troubling reference to the city during non-stop media coverage of the BP oil spill in the Gulf of Mexico in 2010. Just as unpleasant was the occasional mention of the Big Greasy. **See: Big Easy, Chocolate City**

NEW ORLEANIAN (or LIN ee an) One who lives in, or is from New Orleans. **See: Louisianan**

CITY SEAL ALTERNATE VERSION
New Orleans City Hall
1300 Perdido Street – Back O'Town

NEW ORLEANS CITY SEAL Here is evidence of alternate realities. The 31 stars on the official seal apparently represent the first states admitted into the Union as of 1850. The Indian brace and maiden stand on each side of a shield representing the first inhabitants of the New Orleans area. The shield hosts a recumbent nude figure saluting the sun rising over mountains. Some people say the mountains are wigwams and others suggest that the figure is that of Neptune representing Father Mississippi. Some have argued that the sun's rays represent the warm climate of the city. What I can tell you for sure is that there an alligator at the bottom of the seal – or is it a crocodile? **See: Louisiana State Seal**

NINTH WARD The Ninth Ward, often pronounced (Nint' Ward), is the largest and best known of the seventeen New Orleans wards. It stretches from the Mississippi River to Lake Pontchartrain and is bisected by the Industrial Canal. The Upper Ninth includes the neighborhoods of Bywater, St. Claude and the Desire/Florida area. The Lower Ninth, east of the canal, is called the "Lower Nine" and includes the historic neighborhood of Holy Cross as well as Jackson Barracks. Fats Domino is from the Lower Nine. The entire expanse of New Orleans East is also part of the Ninth Ward but is never referred to as such. **See: Bywater, Industrial Canal, Little Woods, The East, Versailles**

NOCCA (NO ka) is an acronym for the New Orleans Center for the Creative Arts located in Bywater. NOCCA provides intensive training in the arts to Louisiana's high school students. **See: Bywater, SUNO, UNO**

NOMA (NO ma) The New Orleans Museum of Art was originally known as the Isaac Delgado Art Museum in City Park. **See: Delgado**

NOPD is the abbreviation for the New Orleans Police Department. The NOPD patch is very similar to the seal of New Orleans.

NOPSI (NOP see) New Orleans Public Service Inc. once operated local utilities and public transportation. Those duties have been taken over by Entergy and the Regional Transit Authority (RTA), respectively. You still hear locals refer to their electric bill as the NOPSI bill. **See: RTA, Trouble Wagon**

NORA The New Orleans Redevelopment Authority was formerly called The Community Improvement Agency. It supports neighborhood recovery projects and economic redevelopment.

NORCO (NOR co) is an oil refining town in St. Charles Parish. The name is an acronym for the New Orleans Refining Company. **See: Lapalco**

NORD was the pre-Katrina acronym for the New Orleans Recreation Department. It is now known as NORDC, The New Orleans Recreation Development Commission.

NORENA (nor EE na) is the unofficial nickname for the New Orleans Arena located next to the Superdome. It is home to the New Orleans Pelicans. **See: Superdome, VooDoo**

NORTH SHORE Generally speaking, the North Shore refers to St. Tammany Parish and the communities of Mandeville, Covington, Madisonville, Abita Springs, Lacombe, Eden Isles and Slidell. As a geographic reference in relation to New Orleans and Lake Pontchartrain, it should be written as two words. However, it has become a specific region of the state and many businesses and subdivisions use one word: Northshore. **See: Causeway, Ozone Belt, West Bank**

NOTTOWAY (NOT away) Plantation is the largest of the antebellum plantations remaining in Louisiana. It is located on River Road in White Castle, Louisiana, just south of Baton Rouge. Nottoway is Algonquin for rattlesnake. It is routinely misspelled Nottaway, or worse:

The streets in the Lake Bullard subdivision are named for plantations and this one is officially misspelled: Notaway. **See: Antebellum**

NOUPT is an acronym for the New Orleans Union Passenger Terminal located between the CBD and Central City. It is the terminus for Amtrak service. We simply refer to it as the train station.

NOWFE is an acronym for The New Orleans Wine and Food Experience. Each year in May, over thirty dinners take place at various restaurants at the same time all around New Orleans.

NUTRIA is a very pesky rodent imported from South America by the McIlhenny family for its fur and easily identified by its bright orange-yellow teeth. Now, they are everywhere and eating up our wetlands. Some refer to it as a "nutr'a rat" but it is really a coypu. Some folks actually enjoy eating them. The late Jefferson Parish Sheriff, Harry Lee, enjoyed shooting them. I'm with Harry. **See: Avery Island, Tabasco**

MR. OKRA'S NEW TRUCK
Frenchmen Street - Faubourg Marigny
April 2012

O IS FOR OYSTERS ROCKEFELLER

OBITUARY COCKTAIL is a captivating mixture of gin, dry vermouth and absinthe customarily poured at Lafitte's Blacksmith Shop on Bourbon Street. **See: Lafitte, Pimm's Cup, Sazerac**

OCHSNER (OX ner)   This is the correct way to pronounce the name of the Ochsner Medical Center in Jefferson Parish. It is often misspelled Ocshner. The hospital was co-founded by Dr. Alton Ochsner, one of the first to document the link between cancer and cigarettes. It is commonly pronounced (OSH ner) which has gained acceptance but is technically incorrect.

OLD RIVER CONTROL STRUCTURE is a floodgate system near Point Breeze, Louisiana, designed to prevent the Mississippi River from being captured by the Atchafalaya River Basin. The word Old does not indicate that there is a New River Control Structure. The Old River is the actual name of the channel that is a former loop of the Mississippi River.
See: Atchafalaya, Morganza

ONZAGA STREET (on ZA ga)   Luis de Unzaga was Governor of Louisiana from 1770-1777, but his name will be misspelled in the street tiles of New Orleans forever.
See: Almonaster

OPELOUSAS (ah puh LOO sus)   This city in St. Landry Parish served as state capital for nine months during the Civil War and is now known as the Zydeco Capital of the World. Opelousas also plays host to the annual International Cajun Joke Telling Contest. It is Choctaw for black legs.
See: Zydeco

OPP The initials on those ubiquitous orange jumpsuits stand for Orleans Parish Prison which is operated by the Orleans Parish Sheriff's Office. **See: Central Lock Up, Tulane and Broad**

ORLEANS PARISH (or LEENS) Unlike the City of New Orleans (OR luns); the parish and street are pronounced (or LEENS). Incidentally, the City of New Orleans and Orleans Parish are coterminous. I mention this because I like to say: coterminous. **See: New Orleans, Parish**

PEARL RESTAURANT AND OYSTER BAR
119 St. Charles Avenue - CBD

OYSTERS ROCKEFELLER is a specialty oyster dish created by Antoine's in the French Quarter. The dish was named after John D. Rockefeller, the richest American at the time. The secret recipe includes a combination of oysters, capers, parsley and parmesan cheese topped with a rich white sauce of butter, flour and milk. Again, this is a secret recipe so please do not repeat this. **See: Crawfish, Shrimp**

OUACHITA (WASH i ta) is a parish located in North Louisiana and is often misspelled Washita. The parish seat is Monroe. **See: North Louisiana, Parish**

OVEN vaults are rows of bricked burial crypts that form the walls of most of the historic New Orleans cemeteries. Their arch shape resembles a baker's oven. **See: All Saints Day, Cemeteries**

OZONE BELT refers to the Covington/Abita Springs region of the North Shore where the air is fresh and the water pure as ... wait a minute. The dictionary says that ground-level ozone is a faint blue irritating air pollutant with a characteristic pungent odor having harmful effects on the respiratory system of humans ... Gulp! **See: Abita Springs, North Shore, Tangipahoa**

TOUCHDOWN JESUS
St. Anthony's Garden - French Quarter
December 2005 - Katrina Damage

P IS FOR PIROGUE

PAIN PERDU (PAHN per DOO) is the New Orleans version of French toast, literally meaning lost bread. It was traditionally made from stale French bread and served for breakfast. **See: French Bread, Perdido**

PANNÉED VEAL (PAH NAYD) is the traditional New Orleans term for breaded veal cutlet. It is sometimes spelled with one N. **See: Grillades**

PARADIS (PAHR uh dee) This city in St. Charles Parish is not to be confused with the city of Paradise in Rapides Parish. **See: Rapides**

PAIR OF BEADS I was standing next to a tourist at the Bacchus parade one year when she turned to me and shouted, "I caught a necklace!" It actually took a few seconds to realize what she meant. By the way, it's not a string of beads either! If you drive down St. Charles Avenue after Mardi Gras, you will see that beads actually grow on trees! **See: Doubloon Reflex, Throw**

PARIS ROAD This Chalmette thoroughfare is often called Parish Road because it is in da Parish. Also known as Interstate 510; it connects lower St. Bernard Parish with Interstate 10 in New Orleans East. It was originally intended to connect to a city called Paris on the Lakefront. There is a Paris Avenue in Orleans Parish further complicating things. **See: da Parish, Green Bridge**

PARISH The state of Louisiana is divided into sixty-four parishes, not counties. Catholic Church parish boundaries played an important role in local politics and government. Accordingly, state civil districts throughout Louisiana became known as parishes. **See: da Parish**

PARK ISLAND A small residential island on Bayou St. John between St. Bernard Avenue and City Park. **See: Devil's Elbow**

PARRAINE (pah RAHN) is a local reference to one's godfather. **See: Marraine**

Pascal's Manale Restaurant Inc.
SINCE 1913 — HOME of THE ORIGINAL B-B-Q SHRIMP —

PASCAL'S MANALE The unusual name for this Creole-Italian restaurant is the result of Manale's Restaurant on Napoleon Avenue being purchased by his nephew Pascal Radosta. Pascal's Manale is famous for its barbecued shrimp and oyster bar. **See: Shrimp**

PASS A GOOD TIME is a Cajun expression for having fun. If you attend a cochon de lait, you will "pass a good time." **See: Cochon de Lait**

PASSION MARK You know that red mark on your neck after a bit of passion; it's not a hickey. It's a passion mawk, dawlin'. **See: Hickey**

PAVILION OF THE TWO SISTERS This pavilion in the City Park Botanical Garden, built in the style of an orangery, is available to rent for parties and weddings. It was named for Miss Erminia Wadsworth and Mrs. Marian Wadsworth Harvey. Not to be confused with the Court of Two Sisters or Two Sisters Restaurant. **See: Court of Two Sisters**

PECAN (puh KAWN) is a nut, indigenous to the South, used in pies and pralines. If you ask someone in New Orleans for a (PEE can) they will think you are looking for a portable restroom. **See: Praline**

PENISTON STREET (PEN is ton) I have watched many news anchors mispronounce this Uptown street in the teleprompter unawares. It was named for Dr. Thomas Peniston. Take the high road. **See: Uptown**

PENSION TOWN is an old-timer's reference to what is currently known as the Leonidas neighborhood in the Carrollton area, aka, Pigeon Town. **See: Leonidas**

PERDIDO STREET (per DEE dough)   This street in the CBD is derived from the Spanish word for lost or to lose. New Orleans City Hall is located on Perdido Street - any questions? **See: CBD, Pain Perdu**

PEYCHAUD'S BITTERS (PAY SHOWED)   Pharmacist Antoine Peychaud, originally from Santa Domingo, brought his family recipe for aromatic bitters to New Orleans. The preparation of bitters was originally believed to have medicinal properties and became the basis for the original New Orleans cocktail - the Sazerac. It is also used in a Manhattan and an Old Fashioned. **See: Herbsaint, Sazerac**

PHUNNY PHORTY PHELLOWS   Phun, phrivolity and a traditional streetcar ride by this organization officially usher in the Carnival season on the evening of January 6th. King Cake is served and custom dictates that whoever gets the slices containing the Carnival babies are declared Queen and Boss Phellow for the year. The ride starts at the streetcar barn in Carrollton. **See: King Cake, Streetcar Barn, Twelfth Night**

PICAYUNE (pick ee YOON) is a Spanish coin worth about six and a quarter cents. It is also the name of our once daily newspaper, *The Times-Picayune*. Picayune refers to something small or insignificant which is appropriate since *The Times-Picayune* plans to cut back to three issues a week. It is also the name of a small town in Mississippi. **See: Lagniappe**

PIGEON TOWN is a section of West Carrollton, also known as Leonidas, located west of the intersection of South Claiborne and South Carrollton Avenues.   **See: Leonidas, Pension Town**

PILOTLAND Written as one word, Pilotland is one of the twenty-two neighborhoods that make up the Gentilly District. It is located along St. Bernard Avenue just north of I-610 and east of City Park. **See: Gentilly Ridge, St. Bernard Projects**

PILOTTOWN Also written as one word, this small town in Plaquemines Parish is located on the Mississippi River a few miles above Head of Passes. It was once known as Balize. The Bar Pilots guide ships between the Gulf of Mexico up to Pilottown. The Crescent City Port Pilots guide ships from Pilottown upriver to New Orleans. These pilots actually transfer on and off moving ships by way of pilot boats.
See: Head of Passes, Plaquemines

PIMM'S CUP This cocktail is the house specialty at the Napoleon House in the French Quarter. It is made with Pimm's No. 1, a British gin-based beverage. It is mixed with lemonade, a splash of lemon-lime soda and a cucumber garnish. **See: Hurricane, Obituary Cocktail, Sazerac**

PINES VILLAGE This early neighborhood developed in New Orleans East just east of the Industrial Canal was not named for the pine tree but for Sigmund Pines, a developer.
See: Indian Village, Musician's Village

PIRATES ALLEY This one block passageway between the St. Louis Cathedral and the Cabildo was formerly called Orleans Alley. **See: Dutch Alley, Jean Lafitte**

PIROGUE (PEE row) or (PEE rogue) A pirogue is the Cajun version of a canoe which is traditionally hollowed out of a solid cypress log; perfect for negotiating the Louisiana swamps. Today they may be made of plywood or fiberglass. **See: Cajun**

PITOT HOUSE (PEE toe) The historic home of James Pitot is located on Moss Street on Bayou St. John. He was the first mayor of the incorporated city of New Orleans, 1804-05.

PLACE D'ARMES (plas D'ARM) This is an older French reference to what is now Jackson Square. It was a military parade ground in the 18th century. **See: Italian Plaza, Jackson Square**

Quaint Essential New Orleans

PLACE JOHN PAUL DEUX One block of Chartres Street between St Louis Cathedral and Jackson Square is named in honor of Pope John Paul II's visit to New Orleans in 1987. **See: Chartres**

PLAQUEMINE (PLAK uh min) or (PLAK min) is a city in Iberville Parish named for its proximity to Bayou Plaquemine. The bayou was named for the persimmon trees along its banks. Pikamine was the Native American word for persimmon, which they used in bread making. Notice the difference in the spelling of the parish.

PLAQUEMINES (PLAK minz) or (PLAK uh minz) is a parish in extreme southeast Louisiana. When entering Plaquemines Parish there are two welcome signs; one spelled without the S. Looka!

Quaint Essential New Orleans

PO-BOY (POE boy) The quintessential New Orleans sandwich is available in many variations from fried shrimp to sloppy roast beef - always served on crispy French bread. In fact, it is the bread that differentiates it from heroes or submarines. It is often written as po' boy. Some bakeries and restaurants (Liuzza's) use the term "poor boy" but we rarely pronounce it that way. "Dawlin', you want dat dressed, or what?" **See: Barq's, Dressed, French Bread**

POINT A LA HACHE (POINT la HASH) or (Point a la HASH) is a village in Plaquemines Parish. It is also common to see it spelled with all capital initials: Point A La Hache and sometimes hyphenated. Hache means chopped or axe.
See: Plaquemines

POINTE AUX HERBES (PWAN oh AHHB) Also known as South Point; this is a region of New Orleans East where Highway 11 and I-10 intersect, just before they cross Lake Pontchartrain toward Slidell. **See: Gumbo Z'herbes, Irish Bayou, Twin Spans**

POINTE COUPEE (PWENT koo PAY) or (POINT koo PEE) According to the Parish's website, both pronunciations are acceptable and it is often misspelled Point Coupe. Iberville and Bienville discovered this point where the Mississippi River doubled back on itself forming an oxbow. This site was named "la Pointe Coupee" or the place of the cut off. **See: Cut Off**

POLYMNIA STREET (puh LIM nee ya) This street in New Orleans was named for the Muse Polyhymnia.
See: Clio, Melpomene, Terpsichore

PONCHATOULA (pon cha TOO la) This city in Tangipahoa Parish is the indisputable Strawberry Capital of the World. It is the Choctaw word for flowing or hanging hair describing the abundance of moss hanging from the trees. Be careful with spelling. **See: Spanish Moss, Tangipahoa**

Quaint Essential New Orleans

"PONCHATULA" STRAWBERRIES
The Strawberry Capital of the World
November 2006

LAKE PONTCHARTRAIN

Traveled on by Iberville, 1699 and named for the French Minister of Marine. Indians called it Okwa-ta, wide water. First port of embarkation was at the site where Bayou St. John flows from this lake. It was the first water travel route to the City of New Orleans.

PONTCHARTRAIN (PON chuh train) is the largest lake in Louisiana and the second largest brackish or salt-water lake in the United States. The lake is named for Louis Phélypeaux, Comte de Pontchartrain, who was the French Minister of Marine under Louis XIV. The name is constantly misspelled without the first T as seen on this neutral ground marker in the CBD. **See: Causeway, Ponchatoula, Twin Spans**

PONTCHARTRAIN BEACH was the name of the former amusement park located at Milneburg or the north terminus of Elysian Fields Avenue. **See: Milneburg, Zephyr**

PONTCHARTRAIN EXPRESS is a proposed passenger ferry service crossing Lake Pontchartrain from West End to Mandeville. **See: West End**

PONTCHARTRAIN EXPRESSWAY is a section of Interstate 10 that runs from the I-610 split in Lakeview to the Crescent City Connection. Not to be confused with the Lake Pontchartrain Causeway. **See: Causeway, Interstate 10**

PONTILLY is a neighborhood association that is a combination of the Pontchartrain Park and Gentilly Woods neighborhoods. **See: Gentilly Ridge**

POO VEIN   I'm not sure how to approach this ...
The next time you order a shrimp cocktail at Deanie's, ask the waitress if they remove the poo veins and let me know what she tells you. By the way, my mother uses a cuticle stick and it works just fine. **See: Shrimp**

POPP FOUNTAIN and **BANDSTAND**   These popular landmarks in City Park are named for benefactor John Popp. Pop's Fountain is incorrect. **See: Alférez**

PORT FOURCHON (FOO shon) This small port community is on the southern tip of Lafourche Parish on the Gulf of Mexico. Its proximity to the LOOP makes it a significant part of the offshore petroleum industry.
See: Lafourche, LOOP

PORT SULPHUR is a town located on the West Bank in Plaquemines Parish. Its name was derived from the Freeport Sulfur Company even though the spelling differs. Not to be confused with the city of Sulphur in Calcasieu Parish.
See: Sulphur

POTTER'S FIELD Holt Cemetery, also called Potter's Field, is the city's burial ground for the indigent. It is located just west of Delgado Community College. There are many unmarked graves as well as many colorful handmade tombstones and crosses. **See: Cemeteries**

POWERS JUNCTION is the traditional designation for the intersection of Highways 11 and 90 in New Orleans East. Robert and Nell Powers operated a restaurant and gas station there called Powers Junction. Not to be confused with Power Boulevard in Kenner. **See: Chef Menteur, White Kitchen**

PRALINE (praw LEEN) This popular local candy is made with pecans, sugar and butter. Pronouncing it (PRAY leen) anywhere near New Orleans is as bad as saying (CRAY fish) or (PEE can). **See: Crawfish, Pecan**

PRINCE OF MARDI GRAS The one and only, Pete Fountain **See: Mardi Gras, Walking Club**

Quaint Essential New Orleans

PRO BONO PUBLICO "For the good of the public" is the motto of Rex. **See: Rex**

PROJECTS or da Projects is the generic reference to any government subsidized housing complex in New Orleans. **See: Calliope, Desire, Iberville, Lafitte, Magnolia, Melpomene, River Garden.**

THE EMPEROR HOLDING COURT
Ernie K-Doe Tomb - St Louis Cemetery #2
All Saints Day 2006 - Tremé

R IS FOR RIGOLETS

RAPIDES (ruh PEEDZ) is a parish in Central Louisiana

CLEVER DISGUISE
Rault Center Hotel - Summer 2005

RAULT CENTER The tragedy at the Rault Center is forever etched in the collective minds of every New Orleanian who watched TV coverage of the horrible fire that raced through the top floors of this sixteen-story building in the CBD. At the time, November 1972, there were no sprinkler systems required in tall buildings. The term itself is a local synonym for a skyscraper fire. **See: Ho Jo Massacre**

RAYNE (RAIN) is a city in Acadia Parish. It is the Frog Capital of the World - not just Louisiana - the World! The annual Frog Festival includes a frog jumping contest. In the unlikely event that you forget to bring your frog, you can rent one!

RED BEANS & RICE is traditional New Orleans comfort food. Legend has it that Creoles did their laundry on Monday with a pot of red beans slowly cooking on the stove. They would throw in any leftover meat from weekend meals. Many neighborhood restaurants offer red beans and rice as a Monday lunch or dinner special. They are usually served with sausage, ham or a pork chop. Louis Armstrong often signed autographs, "Red Beans and Rice-ly Yours." **See: Creole, Lucky Beans**

RED DRINK is a local reference to Barq's Red Crème Soda or any strawberry soda. Here are the general rules: If you order a red drink you will get a Crème Soda; if you just order a Barq's you will get a root beer. **See: Barq's**

RED GRAVY We do not call it tomato sauce in New Orleans. It's "red gravy," - you know - everyone's favorite beverage.

REMOULADE SAUCE (REM a lawd) This classic French sauce is based on oil or mayonnaise. It takes on a uniquely New Orleans flavor with the addition of Tabasco and various Cajun seasonings. It is basically mayonnaise, Creole mustard, horseradish, pickle juice, paprika, garlic and Tabasco and generally used as a seafood dipping sauce. **See: Cocktail Sauce, Creole Mustard, Tabasco, Tony's**

REX is known as the King of Carnival and the Monarch of Merriment. The Rex parade on Mardi Gras is the highlight of the Carnival season. The Rex organization is officially known as the School of Design and was organized in 1872. Rex is Latin for King and the monarch is referred to simply as Rex. King Rex is redundant, as is King of Rex. **See: Carnival, Doubloon, Lundi Gras, Mardi Gras**

RIGOLETS (RIG uh leez) is a pass that connects Lake Pontchartrain and Lake St. Catherine to Lake Borgne. It forms the boundary between New Orleans and St. Tammany Parish. Rigolets comes from the word rigole, French for channel or furrow. Fort Pike, located at the entrance to the Rigolets, was constructed in 1818 to protect New Orleans from another British invasion. The bridge that crosses the Rigolets at Highway 90 is called the Fort Pike Bridge. Not to be confused with Bayou Rigolettes south of Jean Lafitte. **See: Borgne, Chef Menteur, Lake Catherine**

RINGOLD is a street in the Lakeview neighborhood.

RINGGOLD is a town in Bienville Parish named for Major Samuel Ringgold. Note the difference in the spelling of the Lakeview street. **See: Parish**

RIVERBEND refers to the neighborhood surrounding the Uptown intersection of St. Charles and Carrollton Avenues. **See: Carrollton**

RIVERFRONT STREETCAR The red streetcars that run along the riverfront and Canal Street are modern air-conditioned versions of the historic green cars that run along St. Charles Avenue. **See: Streetcar**

RIVER GARDEN is a mixed income development, located just downriver from the Irish Channel. River Garden replaced the old St. Thomas Housing Projects. **See: Irish Channel, Projects**

RIVER PARISHES St. Charles, St. James and St. John the Baptist Parishes are known as the River Parishes. These parishes, sometimes including Ascension Parish, span both banks of the Mississippi River between New Orleans and Baton Rouge. The area is famous for its historic plantation homes. St. Charles and St. John the Baptist parishes also make up an area called the German Coast. **See: Florida Parishes, German Coast**.

RIVERVIEW PARK Better known as the Butterfly or "The Fly," this park is located on the banks of the Mississippi River behind the Audubon Zoo. The name "The Fly" resulted from an old park shelter that had wings resembling a butterfly. **See: Casino**

RIVERWALK Marketplace is a linear shopping complex located along the Mississippi River in the Warehouse District. It should be written as one word. It was the site of a major shipping accident when the cargo ship Bright Field lost power in 1996. **See: Moonwalk, Spanish Plaza**

ROMAN CANDY MAN Sam Cortese's mule-drawn cart has been a New Orleans icon for generations. The Roman Candy Man sells hand-pulled Italian taffy which comes in three flavors: chocolate, vanilla and strawberry. **See: Lucky Dogs**

ROMAN CANDY MAN
Audubon Zoo Revival - Post-Katrina
March 2006 - Uptown

ROSA PARK This semi-private street in the Audubon neighborhood was the first residential park in New Orleans. It has no connection with civil rights pioneer Rosa Parks.

ROUX (REW) "First you make a roux." A roux is a 1:1 mixture of flour and butter - "roux buerre" - that is cooked slowly on a low to medium fire and constantly stirred. It is the base for many New Orleans and Louisiana dishes, primarily gumbo. The darker the roux the more flavor. Making a roux can be tricky and requires some practice in order to avoid burning it. **See: Gumbo, Rue**

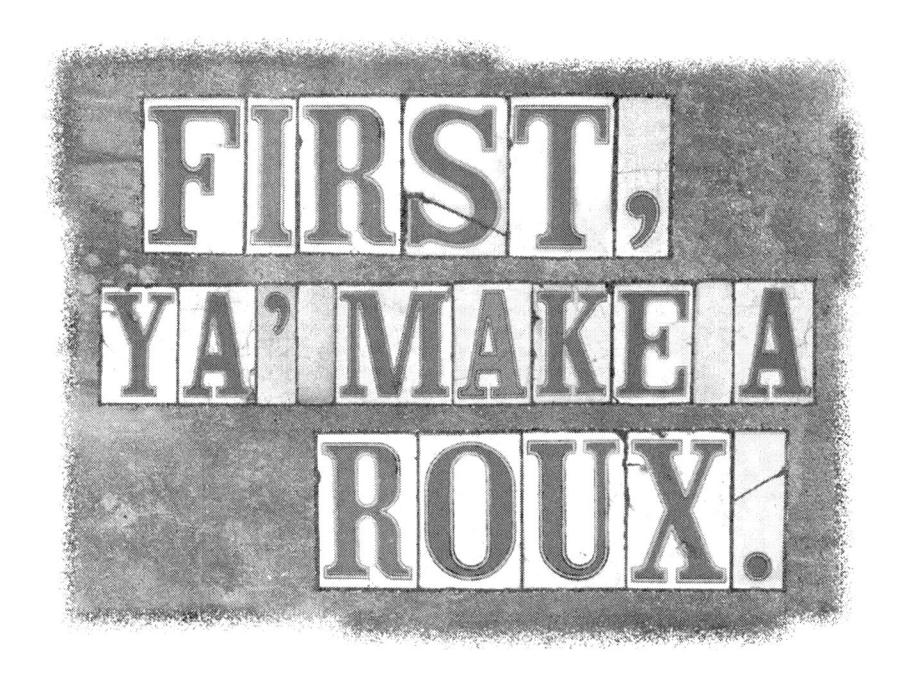

RSD is an acronym for the Recovery School District which was formed by the Louisiana Department of Education following Hurricane Katrina. **See: LRA**

RTA is an acronym for the Regional Transit Authority which operates the New Orleans transit system including bus lines and the streetcars. **See: Streetcar, NOPSI**

RUE (REW) is the French word for street. It can still be seen on signs in the French Quarter and other historic districts. **See: Calle, Roux**

Quaint Essential New Orleans

THE ANGEL INTERCESSOR
St. Roch Cemetery - Faubourg St. Roch
July 2006 - Katrina Waterline

S IS FOR SAZERAC

SAENGER THEATRE This historic 1927 theatre located on Canal Street was completely renovated in 2013. Listed here for spelling which seems to be a constant problem in the press.
See: Broadway South

ST. AUGUSTINE (uh GUS tin) or (AW gus teen) St. Augustine Church, one of the oldest Roman Catholic churches in New Orleans, is located in Faubourg Tremé.
St. Augustine High School, or Saint Aug, is an all-boys parochial school located in the Seventh Ward of New Orleans. The Purple Knights are famous for their marching band known as the Marching 100. Most locals use the second pronunciation, however graduates of the school insist on (uh GUS tin). **See: Creole, Tremé**

ST. BERNARD PROJECTS This housing project in the Pilotland neighborhood of New Orleans was located along St. Bernard Avenue. It was not in St. Bernard Parish. The entire development was razed after Katrina to make way for a new mixed income community called Columbia Parc.
See: Pilotland, Projects

ST. HELENA (hell EE na) is one of the Florida Parishes.
See: Florida Parishes

ST. JOHN'S EVE The evening of June 23rd marks the celebration before the Feast Day of St. John the Baptist. Historically, this date is important in the practice of Voodoo. Marie Laveau is said to have held ritualistic ceremonies on the banks of Bayou St. John at the Wishing Spot. **See: Wishing Spot, Voodoo**

ST. JOSEPH'S DAY The Feast of St. Joseph, March 19th, is celebrated in many ways within the culture of New Orleans. Sicilian immigrants brought their custom of building St. Joseph's Day altars to the city in the late 19th century in thanks for favors granted. These elaborate public and private altars include displays of food, candles, medals and statuary. The food is distributed to the poor. There are also St. Joseph's Day parades and Italian marching clubs. In addition, the Mardi Gras Indians make one of their traditional appearances on St. Joseph's Night with a street party and march through Central City. The fun begins at the intersection of Washington Avenue and LaSalle Street at 7 o'clock – be there!
See: Lucky Beans, Mardi Gras Indians, Super Sunday

ST. MARY Parish is located on the coast of south central Louisiana and is mistakenly referred to as St. Mary's Parish.

ST. PATRICK'S DAY, March 17th, takes on a different twist in New Orleans when several parades follow the influences of Carnival. Float riders throw beads, cabbages and potatoes to the crowd. Parades and block parties occur throughout the week in the Irish Channel and Bywater with many events actually overlapping with St. Joseph's Day celebrations. **See: Bywater, Irish Channel, Throw**

ST. ROCH (ROCK) The neighborhood and street in New Orleans were named for the shrine and cemetery of St. Roch. The chapel and shrine were dedicated to the patron saint of good health in thanks for the parish being spared any deaths from yellow fever epidemics in the 1800s. **See: Cemeteries, Yellow Jack**

ST. TAMMANARD is a reference to residents of St. Bernard Parish who evacuated to, and now reside in, St. Tammany Parish since Katrina. **See: Arabian, Chalmation**

SAUVAGE (so VAZH) The Bayou Sauvage National Wildlife Refuge in New Orleans East is often misspelled Savage. It is, in fact, French for savage or wild. **See: Cat Island - NWR, Bayou**

SAZERAC (SA zer ak) The Sazerac is the original cocktail of New Orleans. Local legend is that the drink was first served in an egg cup called a coquetier which eventually morphed into the word cocktail. It is based on rye whiskey and includes bitters from an old recipe of the family of New Orleans pharmacist, Antoine Peychaud. **See: Herbsaint, Obituary Cocktail, Peychaud's Bitters**

SCHWEGMANN'S BAG (SHWEG minz) is a specific unit of measure in New Orleans based on the size of the large brown paper bags once used by Schwegmann's Giant Supermarkets to pack your groceries. It is also known as a Yat suitcase. If you ask the grocer for a "sack" you will just get a blank stare. In some neighborhoods you might hear (SHWAG a minz). "I caught enough beads on Mardi Gras to fill three Shwagaminz bags!" **See: 'Aints, Ain't Dere No More, Bag Heads, Make Groceries, Yat**

SEABROOK BRIDGE is the popular name for the bridge that crosses the Industrial Canal at the lakefront in New Orleans. The official name is the Senator Ted Hickey Bridge. In fact the general area where the canal enters Lake Pontchartrain is referred to as Seabrook including the swimming area and boat launch. **See: Claiborne Bridge, Industrial Canal**

SEABROOK PLACE is the name of the Gentilly neighborhood that runs along the northern end of Franklin Avenue between Filmore Avenue and Leon C. Simon Drive. **See: Filmore**

SEAWALL refers to the 1920s era cement steps that run the length of the lakefront from the Industrial Canal to West End. It is sometimes called the Lake Pontchartrain steps.

The seawall provides a breakwater to protect the lakefront neighborhoods from high storm waves and erosion. It is also a traditional place to go fishing and crabbing on the lakefront.
See: Crab Trap, Seabrook, West End

SECOND LINE is a spontaneous parade created by onlookers that develops around a main line or a scheduled parade or event. Brass bands, social aid and pleasure clubs and even the Mardi Gras Indians often generate a second line of participants when they march through the neighborhood. Second liners dance along the route traditionally carrying umbrellas and waving handkerchiefs.

The term can also be used as a verb. Audience members at Jazz Fest venues will often second line through the crowd.
See: Benson Boogie, Jazz Funeral, Mardi Gras Indians

SEGNETTE (sig NET) is a bayou and state park in Westwego. **See: Bayou, Westwego**

SEVENTEENTH STREET CANAL The 17th Street Canal, or the Metairie Relief Outfall Canal, runs along the boundary between Orleans and Jefferson Parishes. It allows for the drainage of rain water into Lake Pontchartrain. The canal is not named for 17th Street in Metairie. It actually begins in the back of Carrollton and runs along Palmetto Street which used to be 17th Street.

A breach in a section of the 17th Street Canal floodwall in Lakeview caused much of the city's flooding after Hurricane Katrina. **See: Hammond Highway**

SEWERAGE & WATER BOARD is sometimes seen in print incorrectly as the Sewage & Water Board - and they hate it when that happens. **See: Dock Board**

SHAKSPEARE Joseph A. Shakspeare was mayor of New Orleans in the latter 1880s. The unusual spelling of his name would not sit well with The Bard.

SHEEPHEAD STREET, found among other fish streets in New Orleans East, defies the conventional spelling of sheepshead. It appears as sea bream on some touristy menus, but we know better. **See: Buffalo Road, Choupique, Deers**

SHOO SHOO A firework that fails to explode.

SHOOT-THE-CHUTE In New Orleans, kids don't play on a slide - they slide down the "shoot-the-chute." Sometimes written as: chute-da-chute. **See: Grandma Beads**

SHOTGUN HOUSE A shotgun house typically has one room leading into the next with no hallways, providing little privacy. The old saying is that if a shotgun were fired through the front door, the pellets would go right out the back door. Although a bit of an exaggeration, the layout is appropriate for the New Orleans climate as a good breeze can flow unobstructed through the length of the house. There is a multi-family version known as a 'shotgun double.'
See: Camelback

SHOW The movies, as in: "Let's go to the show!"

SHRIMP is singular and plural, however in some neighborhoods you might hear: "Hey dere's only six shrimps in my cocktail!" Just let it alone. It can be seen as "chevrettes" on some fancy French menus. **See: Cocktail Sauce, Pascal's Manale, Poo Vein, Remoulade Sauce**

Quaint Essential New Orleans

SIMON BOLIVAR (SY mon BAHL a var) This New Orleans street is named for the liberator of several South American countries. It runs through Central City and is often called Simon Boulevard in error.

SKULL AND BONE GANG The mysterious North Side Skull and Bone Gang appears on the streets of Tremé on Mardi Gras around six in the morning. Bone Men, wearing oversize papier-mâché skull masks and hand-drawn skeleton suits, carry ham bones and shout "Wake up!" or "You next!"
See: Baby Dolls, Mardi Gras Indians

SLAVE QUARTERS refers to any small building apart from the main building that housed the servants.

SLIVER BY THE RIVER is that section of New Orleans closest to the Mississippi River which escaped most of the flooding after Hurricane Katrina. The neighborhoods of Bywater, French Quarter, Marigny and upriver to parts of Carrollton, are built on a natural levee system created from hundreds of years of the Mississippi overflowing and creating a ridge of sediment. **See: Batture Dwellers, Gentilly Ridge, Marigny**

SNO-BALL In the 1930s, the Hansen family of New Orleans invented a machine that shaved ice, creating the truly remarkable sno-ball found here. There is no comparison to snow cones found elsewhere which use crushed ice
See: Huck-A-Buck

SOCIAL AID & PLEASURE CLUB Social aid & pleasure clubs are a significant part of the history of the Tremé and 7th Ward neighborhoods. They originally provided a social safety net for African Americans. These organizations, including Zulu, are now responsible for maintaining the traditions of Tremé including second lining, Mardi Gras Indians, jazz funerals and neighborhood marching bands.
See: Mardi Gras Indians, Second Line

SOCRATES STREET in Algiers is often pronounced in the neighborhood as (SO crates). **See: De Saix**

SOFT SHELL CRAB A fried or broiled soft shell crab is a delicacy in New Orleans. A crab's shell remains paper-thin and soft for less than twelve hours after molting. After being dressed, the entire crab is cooked - shell and all - and best served on a po-boy. Meet me at Mandina's! **See: Dressed, Keeper, Loaded She**

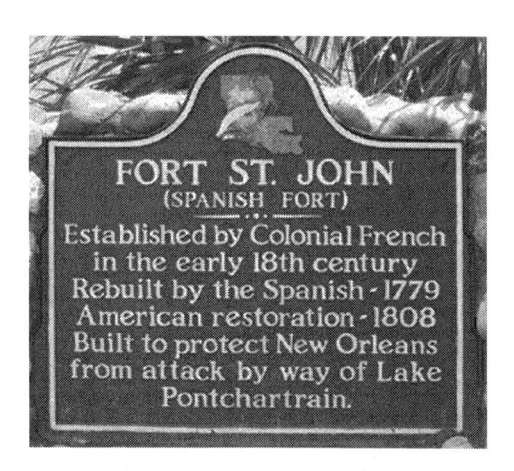

FORT ST. JOHN
(SPANISH FORT)
Established by Colonial French in the early 18th century
Rebuilt by the Spanish - 1779
American restoration - 1808
Built to protect New Orleans from attack by way of Lake Pontchartrain.

SPANISH FORT Old Spanish Fort, as it is known to most locals, sits on Bayou St. John near Lake Pontchartrain. It was once the site of a grand amusement park with restaurants, rides and jazz venues. The actual name of the fort is Fort St. John and it was built to defend New Orleans from an attack by way of Lake Pontchartrain and the bayou. **See: Fort Macomb, Pontchartrain**

Quaint Essential New Orleans

SPANISH MOSS, draped among the branches of the old oak trees in the South, is neither Spanish nor a moss. It is a flowering epiphyte or air plant related to the bromeliad. It is also referred to as Frenchman's wig, Spanish beard and tree hair. **See: Dueling Oaks, Ponchatoula**

SPANISH PLAZA This park, located at the convergence of Canal and Poydras Streets and the Mississippi River, was originally called Eads Plaza. It is ground zero for Lundi Gras activities and serves as a gateway to the Riverwalk Marketplace. **See: Italian Plaza, Moonwalk, Riverwalk**

STOOP generally refers to the front porch of your home where you sit and keep an eye on the neighborhood and chat with passers-by. Traditionally, a stoop was a small set of wooden box steps that led up from the banquette to the entrance of your shotgun. **See: Banquette, Shotgun**

STORYLAND This section of City Park was dedicated in 1956 to the children of New Orleans. Storyland is a fairytale theme park adjacent to City Park's Carousel Gardens and the New Orleans Botanical Garden. Not to be confused with Storyville. **See: Popp Fountain**

STORYVILLE was the legendary red light district where prostitution was legal until 1917. Ironically, Storyville was named for Sidney Story, who fought to have prostitution banned from other neighborhoods in the city. The District was very important in the early development of jazz in New Orleans. The site is now home to the Iberville Housing Project. **See: Blue Book, Iberville, Tango Belt**

STREETCAR The St. Charles Avenue Streetcar Line, since 1835, is the oldest operating street railway in the United States. It is probably one of the only nationally registered historic sites that is never in the same place! The word trolley should never be used in New Orleans when referring to the streetcar. **See: Carrollton Spur, Streetcar Barn, Riverfront Streetcar**

STREETCAR BARN is the common reference to the Carrollton Transit Station at Willow and Dublin Streets. It is the maintenance and storage facility for the St. Charles Avenue Streetcars. It is also ground zero for the annual ride of the Phunny Phorty Phellows on Twelfth Night - the first day of Carnival. **See: Carrollton Spur, Phunny Phorty Phellows, Riverbend**

Quaint Essential New Orleans

SUCK DA HEADS A perfectly acceptable dining ritual while eating boiled crawfish is to break off the head and suck the spicy juices and fat prior to picking the meat from the tail. **See: Crawfish, Don't Eat the Dead Ones**

SULPHUR, a city in Calcasieu Parish, was originally named Sulphur City for the abundance of the element sulfur once extracted from nearby mines. For some reason, the city reflects the British spelling of the element. It is often misspelled Sulpher or Sulfer. **See: Port Sulphur**

SUNO (SUE no) is an acronym for the Southern University of New Orleans. **See: GNO, UNO**

SUPERDOME Though officially called The Mercedes-Benz Superdome, it is commonly referred to simply as the Superdome, the Dome or the New Orleans Superdome. It is a large multi-purpose sports and exhibition facility located in the CBD. Superdome is written as one word unlike Super Bowl. The entire complex including the Superdome and the New Orleans Arena is officially called the John McKeithen Sports and Entertainment Complex in honor of the late Governor of Louisiana. **See: CBD, Norena**

SUPER KREWE The super krewe ushered in a new phase of the Carnival season in the late 1960s. Parades such as Bacchus and Endymion include hundreds of riders on huge floats. Private balls were replaced with public supper dances. These krewes also started the tradition of annual celebrity monarchs. **See: Bacchus, Extravaganza, Krewe**

SUPER SUNDAY This has become an important day in the tradition of the Mardi Gras Indians. Super Sunday usually takes place on a Sunday closest to St. Joseph's Day. The exact series of events is unpredictable. The New Orleans Mardi Gras Indian Council begins its march at A. L. Davis Park. The Tambourine and Fan Club generally assembles on Bayou St. John. **See: Mardi Gras Indians, St. Joseph's Day**

THE FABULOUS CHRIS OWENS
Musical Legends Park - French Quarter
June 2005

T IS FOR TCHOUPITOULAS

TABASCO is practically a synonym for all hot pepper sauces. It is made by the McIlhenny Company of Louisiana from tabasco peppers traditionally grown on Avery Island. Tabasco is capitalized only when referring to the brand name, not the pepper which gets its name from the Mexican state of Tabasco. If you are a true New Orleanian, you can remove and replace the cap from the Tabasco bottle with one hand while swigging an Abita Amber with the other. **See: Avery Island, Nutria**

TABLEAUX pl. (tab LOW) is a series of live-action scenes illustrating the theme of a Carnival parade or ball and portrayed by krewe members at the annual bal masqué before the dancing begins. **See: Ball, Krewe Favor, Mardi Gras**

TANGIPAHOA (tan ji puh HO ah) or (tan ji puh HO) is one of the Florida Parishes north of Lake Pontchartrain. It has become fashionable to simply refer to the area as Tangi (TAN jee). It is the Acolapissa word for corn or corn gatherers. **See: Florida Parishes, North Shore**

TANGO BELT The Tango Belt was in the French Quarter, just a few blocks from Storyville, on North Rampart Street. The Tango Belt had numerous saloons, cabarets, nightclubs and theaters that employed jazz musicians. The name Tango Belt derived from a 1915 newspaper article that used that name to describe this district. In its heyday, the Belt had one of the highest concentrations of jazz venues in the city of New Orleans. **See: Back O'Town, Storyville**

TASSO (TAH so) is thinly sliced strips of highly seasoned smoked pork with a robust flavor. It is a popular seasoning agent for Cajun and southern dishes such as red beans and jambalaya. **See: Andouille, Boudin, Red Beans & Rice**

TCHEFUNCTE RIVER (chuh FUNK tuh) is a tributary of Lake Pontchartrain on the North Shore. It flows past Covington and empties into the Lake Pontchartrain just south of Madisonville. Tchefuncte is Choctaw for chinquapin or chestnut.

There is a medical clinic and subdivision in Covington, Louisiana, which use a variant spelling: Tchefuncta.

TCHOUPITOULAS STREET (chop a TOO lis) One of the longest streets in New Orleans, Tchoupitoulas follows the river crescent from Canal Street to Audubon Park. It is believed to be the Choctaw reference for those who live by the river. An urban legend has it that a police officer reporting a dead horse on Tchoupitoulas couldn't spell it on his police report so he dragged the horse over to Camp Street.

TECHE (TESH) Bayou Teche is a 125-mile long waterway of some cultural significance in south central Louisiana due to its inclusion in Longfellow's poem, *Evangeline*. The word teche is Choctaw for snake. **See: Evangeline**

TERPISCHORE STREET (TERP si core) This street named for the Muse of Music and Dance gets an amusing New Orleans pronunciation. Many Central City residents proudly pronounce it (TERP si coe) **See: Calliope, Clio, Euterpe, Melpomene**

TERREBONNE (TER ah bone) Parish was formed in 1822 from part of Lafourche Parish. The name Terrebonne means good earth. **See: Houma**

> **TERRYTOWN**
> 1960 Paul Kapelow prefab diamond-shaped development with alphabetical street plan named for daughter Terry. Area's "first completely winter-summer air conditioned neighborhood."

TERRYTOWN is an unincorporated area of Jefferson Parish adjacent to the city of New Orleans on the West Bank of the Mississippi River. It was named after the developer's daughter, Terry, and is written as one word. **See: West Bank**

THE EAST is a specific reference to New Orleans East, the vast region of the city that lies to the east of the Industrial Canal, south of Lake Pontchartrain and north of Almonaster Avenue. "He grew up in Gentilly but he now lives in the East." **See: Almonaster, Little Woods, Ninth Ward**

THE POINT is a reference to the terminus of Breakwater Drive on the lakefront in West End. It is the best location in New Orleans to watch submarine races. **See: Algiers Point, West End**

THERIOT (TEH ree oh) is a very small town located in Terrebonne Parish.

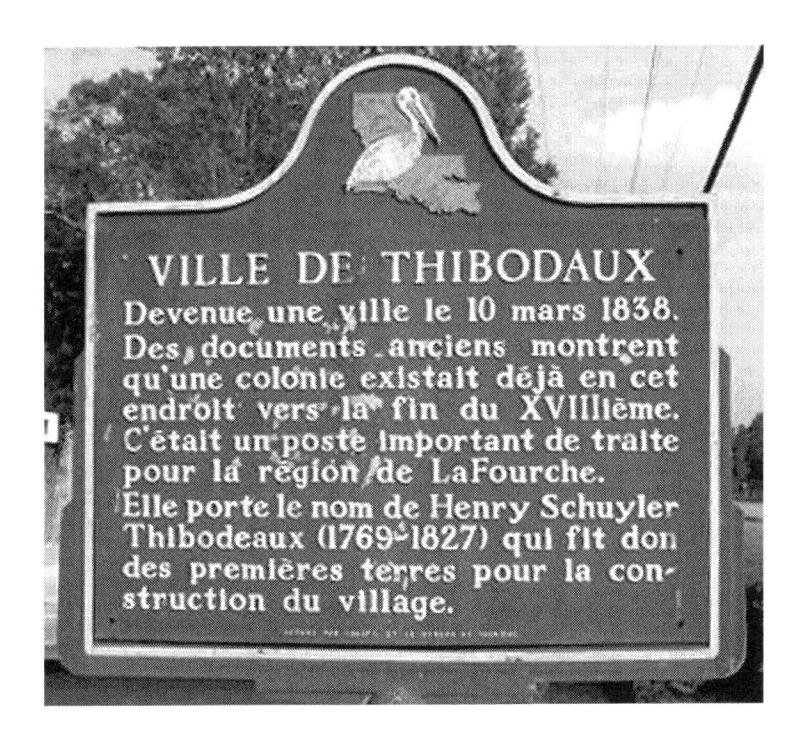

> **VILLE DE THIBODAUX**
> Devenue une ville le 10 mars 1838. Des documents anciens montrent qu'une colonie existait déjà en cet endroit vers la fin du XVIIIième. C'était un poste important de traite pour la région de LaFourche. Elle porte le nom de Henry Schuyler Thibodeaux (1769-1827) qui fit don des premières terres pour la construction du village.

THIBODAUX (TIB uh doe)   This is the correct spelling for the city in Lafourche Parish. The city was spelled like the common Louisiana surname for a while but was changed to the current spelling in 1918. **See: Lafourche**

THIBODEAUX (TIB uh doe) This is the more common spelling of the South Louisiana surname: Thibodeaux. In case this isn't confusing enough, there is a November festival in Thibodaux called the Thibodeauxville Fall Festival which apparently still reflects the old spelling of the city.

THROW   In New Orleans the word "throw" is a noun which refers to any trinket, doubloon or pair of beads tossed to the crowd from a float during Carnival parades and on Mardi Gras. It obviously derives from the traditional expression: "Throw me somethin' mista!" **See: Doubloon, Mardi Gras, Pair of Beads**

[TONI MORRISON INTERCHANGE sign]

TONI MORRISON INTERCHANGE The complicated interchange between Carrollton Avenue, the Pontchartrain Expressway, Airline Highway and Tulane Avenue is not named for the author Toni Morrison. Sorry. It is named for state Rep. DeLesseps Story "Toni" Morrison, son of the former Mayor of New Orleans, "Chep" Morrison.

TONTI (TAHN TEE) This street that runs through downtown New Orleans is named for Henri de Tonti, a companion of La Salle during his Mississippi River explorations. His name is spelled Tonty in some history books. **See: Conti**

TONY'S As in, "Pass the Tony's" - the synonym for any Creole or Cajun seasoning used at the dinner table or while cooking. It refers to Tony Chachere's Creole Seasoning which, incidentally, is available in both regular and travel sizes.
See: Tabasco, Zatarain's

TOUCHDOWN JESUS is an irreverent reference to the beautiful marble statue of the Sacred Heart of Jesus Christ that stands in St. Anthony's Garden located at the rear of St. Louis Cathedral.

TOULOUSE STREET (too LOOSE) Included here for pronunciation and spelling; it was named for the Comte de Toulouse, illegitimate son of Louis XIV.

TOURO STREET (TOUR oh) The hospital and street are named for New Orleans merchant, Judah Touro.
See: A. P. Tureaud

TRADITIONAL ROUTE The standard Carnival parade route in New Orleans begins near Napoleon Avenue, follows St. Charles Avenue to Canal Street and ends either at the Municipal Auditorium or the Morial Convention Center. It is also known as the Uptown Route. **See: Mardi Gras, Municipal Auditorium**

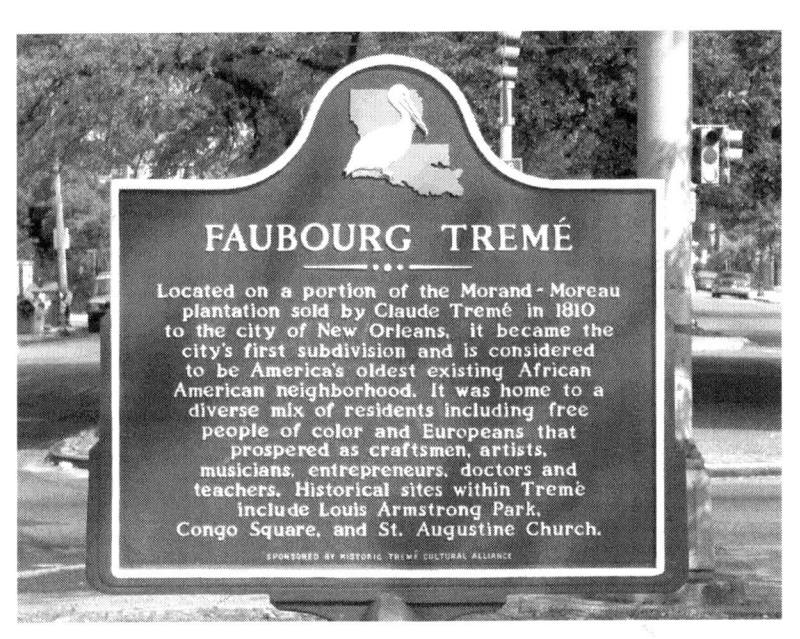

![Faubourg Tremé historical marker]

TREMÉ (tra MAY) Also called Faubourg Tremé, this neighborhood north of the French Quarter has a rich African American history. It was named for Claude Tremé, a landowner. The area includes Armstrong Park and Congo Square. St. Claude Avenue runs through Tremé and was also named for Claude Tremé, who was not a saint. Ironically, the street name was recently changed to Henriette Delille who will soon become a saint. **See: Congo Square, Faubourg**

TREME (TREM ee) Treme is a surname still found in some areas of New Orleans and is not pronounced like neighborhood.

TRICOU STREET (TREE coo) is named for an old New Orleans family.

TROUBLE WAGON "For a safer parade, this 'Krewe' is checking for overhead clearances." Traditionally, a NOPSI cherry picker would precede every parade with this quote and a bamboo pole marking the height of the tallest float to avoid hitting low hanging oak branches. Now it is an Entergy truck. The trouble wagon is always a sure sign that the parade has arrived. **See: Carnival, Krewe, NOPSI**

TUJAGUE'S (TOO jacks) Guillaume Tujague, a French Market butcher and his wife Marie, established Tujague's Restaurant on Decatur Street in the French Quarter in 1856. Try the garlic chicken, it's not on the menu, and share it with the table next to you. Go ahead, it's ok. **See: Pascale's Manale**

TULANE (TOO lane) Avenue and the University, named for Paul Tulane, are pronounced with the accent on the first syllable. Students and sportscasters from out of town, as well as some Uptown residents, pronounce it (too LANE). **See: Uptown**

TULANE AND BROAD is not just an intersection in New Orleans, it is a synonym for the local criminal justice system. It is the location of the Orleans Parish Criminal District Court building, Traffic Court and Parish Prison. The general vicinity is also home to bail bondsmen and lawyers. If you're in a jam at Tulane and Broad, you probably aren't stuck in traffic! **See: Broad Street, OPP**

TWELFTH NIGHT Carnival festivities begins on January 6th, also known as Twelfth Night or Epiphany. One of the city's oldest krewes, The Twelfth Night Revelers, holds a bal masqué to mark the occasion. The leader of the "Revelers" is known as The Lord of Misrule. It is also the night of the traditional streetcar ride by the Phunny Phorty Phellows as well as the official start of King Cake season. **See: Ball, King Cake, Phunny Phorty Phellows**

TWIN SPANS It is neither the "twin span" nor the "twin span bridge" - which is redundant. This is a specific reference to Interstate 10 as it crosses eastern Lake Pontchartrain connecting New Orleans East and Slidell. This is the modern alternative to the old Highway 11 Bridge. It should not be confused with the Lake Pontchartrain Causeway. The Department of Transportation officially refers to the bridges as the I-10 Twin Span Bridge just to irritate the life out of me.
See: Causeway, Highway 11 Bridge

THREE MUSICAL LEGENDS
Musical Legends Park - French Quarter

U IS FOR URSULINES

UGLESICH'S (YOU gla sitch es)   This quintessential New Orleans neighborhood restaurant "Ain't Dere No More."
See: Ain't Dere No More

UGLESICH'S RESTAURANT "CLOSING DAY"
1238 Baronne St. - Central City
May 2005

UNO   In 1974, the name of the Louisiana State University in New Orleans was changed to the University of New Orleans but remains part of the LSU system. When pronouncing the university you spell it out, U-N-O, unlike SUNO which is pronounced: (SUE no). **See: Lakefront Arena, SUNO**

UPTOWN is a general reference for just about everything in New Orleans upriver from Canal Street to Audubon Park including the Garden District, the Irish Channel, Carrollton, as well as Central City.

Uptown is also the name of an official neighborhood bounded by Napoleon and Jefferson Avenues and Magazine and La Salle Streets. This district is also known as Faubourg Bouligny, named for Louis Bouligny's plantation. To most New Orleanians, the term "Uptown" has a much broader scope than the official city designation. **See: Bouligny, Canal Street, Central City, Irish Channel**

UPTOWN TRIANGLE See: Black Pearl

URQUHART STREET (ER kwart) often (ER kart)
Mind your spelling and pronunciation of this New Orleans street that runs through the Bywater and St. Claude neighborhoods. It was named for New Orleans banker, Thomas Urquhart. **See: Bywater**

URSULINES STREET (ER sa line)   This street and avenue in New Orleans were originally called Rue des Ursulines for the nuns that resided at the old Ursuline Convent located in the French Quarter. It should still be written with the final S even though it is not pronounced. The modern street signs are correct but some tiles on the banquette omit the final S.

Please note the exception to the "s" rule when referring to the Ursuline Convent and Ursuline Academy. **See: Rue**

V IS FOR VIEUX CARRÉ

VERMILION (ver MIL yuhn) Vermilion Parish and Bay are spelled with one L. However:

VERMILLION BOULEVARD This boulevard in New Orleans is spelled with a double L even though it was named for the parish. **See: Parish**

VERSAILLES, or Versailles Village, is a Vietnamese community in New Orleans East. The area gets its name from the Versailles Arms, a housing project settled in 1975 by Vietnamese refugees. **See: Little Saigon, Michoud**

Versailles also refers to an area in St. Bernard Parish named for a former plantation. **See: Paris Road**

VIDALIA (vih DAIL yuh) is a town in Concordia Parish. Alas, Vidalia onions are not named for Vidalia, Louisiana, but for Vidalia, Georgia. Does that make you cry?
See: Holy Trinity

VIENNA (vie AN na) is a town in Lincoln Parish. There is not much information explaining the name. It most probably came from settlers who traveled from Vienna, Georgia, since they have the same unusual pronunciation.

> Orleans Ave
> Vieux Carre'
> NEXT RIGHT

VIEUX CARRÉ (vyuh ka RAY) or "old square" is another name for the French Quarter. The French Quarter stretches fourteen blocks along the Mississippi River from Canal Street to Esplanade Avenue and back seven blocks from the Mississippi to Rampart Street. If you are entering the city on I-10 west, look for the French Quarter exit. If you are on I-10 east, look for the Vieux Carré exit. Remember, this is New Orleans. **See: Bonnet Carré, Faubourg**

VILLAGE DE L'EST (vi LAZH de LEST) means Village of the East according to the commercial jingle that touted this new subdivision in the early 1960s. Today it refers to the vast area of New Orleans East extending from Michoud to Lake Catherine. It is home to a vibrant Vietnamese community also known as Versailles. **See: Lake Catherine, Little Saigon, Michoud, Versailles**

VILLE PLATTE (VIL PLAT) is a city in Evangeline Parish once known as Flat Ville or Flat Town. A good Cajun knows to say (VEEL PLOT). It is home to the annual Cajun Gumbo Festival.

VILLERE STREET (VIL a ree) in New Orleans is named for Gen. Jacques P. Villere and not pronounced (vil AIR). **See: Gallier**

Quaint Essential New Orleans

VOODOO (VOO doo) New Orleans Voodoo came from Africa but was modified in Haiti. The practice includes belief in zombies, ghosts and demons with a little Catholicism thrown in. The most influential Voodoo priestess of her time was Marie Laveau, the Voodoo Queen. **See: Gris-Gris, Marie Laveau, St. John's Eve, Wishing Spot**

VOODOO The New Orleans VooDoo is the Arena Football League team based in New Orleans. They play their games in the "Norena." **See: Norena, Zephyrs**

WEST END LIGHTHOUSE
New Basin Canal - West End
July 2005

W, X, Y & Z

WAGGAMAN (WAG uh muhn) is a town in Jefferson Parish named for George Augustus Waggaman; politician and veteran of the War of 1812. His plantation was called Avondale. **See: Avondale, West Bank**

MARDI GRAS FOUNTAIN
Lakeshore Drive – Lakefront - 2004

WALKING CLUB A Walking Club is a roving Mardi Gras celebration made up of maskers and revelers accompanied by Dixieland or brass bands. Some have planned routes and others simply roam the city at will. The goal is to stop at as many bars as possible along the way. The most famous is the Half-Fast Walking Club led by the Prince of Mardi Gras - Pete Fountain. **See: Dixieland, Second Line**

WAREHOUSE DISTRICT The old warehouse district located just upriver from the CBD was created by development spurred on by the 1984 World's Fair. It is now home to swanky restaurants, condos and includes the Arts District. **See: Arts District, CBD, Italian Plaza**

WATER WORKS The general reference to the Carrollton Water Purification Plant located on S. Claiborne Avenue in Pigeon Town. **See: Leonidas**

WEST BANK As a geographic reference, West Bank should be written as two words even though the sign painters disagree with me. Orleans Parish is divided by the Mississippi River, so the neighborhood of Algiers is on the West Bank. However, the term is also used to include suburbs of Jefferson and Plaquemines Parishes across the river from New Orleans such as Waggaman, Avondale, Marrero, Gretna, Harvey, Westwego, Belle Chasse and Terrytown. Residents call it the Best Bank.

When you cross the Crescent City Connection to reach the West Bank you are traveling due east. **See: Belle Chasse, CCC, Plaquemines, Terrytown, Westwego**

WEST END is the neighborhood in New Orleans where the Seventeenth Street Canal meets Lake Pontchartrain. West End was originally called New Lake End differentiating it from Old Lake End - or Milneburg. It was famous for its early jazz clubs and seafood restaurants. **See: Bucktown, Milneburg**

WESTWEGO (west WE go) is a city on the West Bank in Jefferson Parish. As trains departed the station heading west, guess what the conductor yelled?

WHERE Y'AT? A traditional New Orleans greeting equivalent to what's up? ...or how are you? This expression is the origin of the term: Yat. **See: Mom-n-em, Mynez, Yat**

WHITE KITCHEN The junction of Highways 90 and 190, east of the Rigolets, and the surrounding area, is known as White Kitchen. It was the site of the White Kitchen Restaurant which burned down decades ago. Jayne Mansfield was seen eating at the White Kitchen just minutes before her fatal accident a few miles down the road. It is now the location of the White Kitchen Preserve which protects an important swamp system and bald eagle nesting sites. **See: Dead Man's Curve, Powers Junction, Rigolets**

WHITE LINEN NIGHT This annual celebration of the New Orleans art scene is generally held on the first Saturday night in August in the Warehouse District. Linen is regarded as a comfortable fabric to withstand those sultry New Orleans evenings. Of course the jeroboams of Pinot Grigio flowing along Julia Street also help! **See: Dirty Linen Night, Warehouse District**

WHO DAT originally referred to an opponent of the New Orleans Saints. "Who Dat say dey gonna beat dem Saints. Who Dat?" Today Saints fans call themselves Who Dats as in the reference "Who Dat Nation." **See: 'Aints, Bag Heads, Benson Boogie**

WHO KILLA' DA CHIEF? This phrase was a derogatory expression directed at the New Orleans Italian community after the assassination of Police Chief David Hennessy in 1890. **See: Hennessy, Italian Plaza, Little Palermo**

WILL STUTLEY DRIVE In English folklore, one of Robin Hood's Merry Men finds his name spelled Will Stutely or Will Stutly. However, in Sherwood Forest in New Orleans East, we still managed to find a way to misspell it.

WISHING SPOT is a secret spot on Bayou St. John, probably near Lake Pontchartrain, where Marie Laveau held her sensual Voodoo rituals including erotic snake dances and decapitated roosters. It is so secret; I can't tell you where it is. **See: Marie Laveau, Gris-Gris, St. John's Eve**

WISNER (WHYZ ner) is a town in Franklin Parish with a pronunciation differing from the boulevard in New Orleans.

WISNER BOULEVARD (WIZ ner) This boulevard named for Edward Wisner runs along Bayou St. John and City Park. The signs say boulevard but the plaque on the overpass at I-610 reads Wisner Drive. Go figure.

WISTERIA STREET This Gentilly street is spelled Wisteria on the street signs ...

... however, the tiles in the pavement use the variant spelling: Wistaria. **See: Camelia**

WOLDENBERG PARK refers to the linear park along the Mississippi River between the Aquarium of the Americas and the Moonwalk. It was named after Malcolm Woldenberg and his name is constantly misspelled Waldenburg or Woldenburg. **See: Moonwalk**

WOP SALAD is a politically incorrect but traditionally accepted New Orleans reference for Italian or olive salad. The term always appeared on local restaurant menus ever since I can remember. Check out Rocky and Carlo's in Chalmette. **See: Coonass, da Parish, Muffuletta**

WROUGHT IRON is often confused with cast iron. Wrought iron is hammered by hand instead of being cast in a mold. **See: Balcony, Cast Iron, Gallery**

WTC is an acronym for The World Trade Center located at the foot of Canal Street, formerly known as the International Trade Mart. **See: Spanish Plaza**

XAVIER (ZAY vyer) is an African American university in Gert Town, nationally recognized as a training ground for doctors and pharmacists. Also known as XULA. The general area between Washington Avenue and Interstate 10 is known as the Xavier Triangle. It is often mispronounced: (ex A vee yer). **See: Gert Town**

YAT or Y'AT refers to a dialect spoken in New Orleans as well as one who speaks with the Yat accent. The term is derived from a common greeting, "Where Y'at?" It is an exaggerated accent, similar to that heard in Brooklyn, and generally associated with the Ninth Ward of New Orleans. It can also be heard in the Irish Channel and Mid-City, as well as by expatriates living in St. Bernard and St. Tammany Parishes. **See: Mom-n-em, Mynez, N'Awlins, Ninth Ward, St. Tammanard, Where Y'at?**

YELLOW JACK is a dramatic reference to outbreaks of Yellow Fever which were common in New Orleans during the nineteenth century. **See: Mortuary Chapel, St. Roch**

YSCLOSKEY (why CLOS kee) is a community in St. Bernard Parish originally called Proctorville. Keep a close eye on pronunciation and spelling. **See: da Parish**

ZAPP'S Potato Chips are cooked and packaged in Gramercy. They are kettle-cooked in peanut oil. The company was founded by the late Ron Zappe. Their specialty chips are marketed with names like Spicy Cajun Crawtator, Sour Cream and Creole Onion, and Cajun Dill Gator-tators.
See: Gramercy

ZATARAIN'S (ZAT uh rans) Originally a Gretna company producing root beer, Zatarain's is now a major local producer of spices and assorted Cajun and Creole food products. It has become a synonym for boiling spices as in, "add some more Zatarain's to the crab boil." **See: Crawfish, Creole Mustard, Tony's**

ZEPHYR   This historic and very popular wooden roller coaster at Pontchartrain Beach was razed after the Beach closed in 1983; along with Zephyr Jr. **See: Pontchartrain Beach, Lincoln Beach**

ZEPHYRS   The local PCL baseball team is the New Orleans Zephyrs. Can you imagine any other city in America choosing a nutria as its mascot? **See: Nutria, VooDoo**

ZIMPEL STREET (ZIM pul) in Uptown New Orleans is named for Charles Zimpel. The street is often misspelled Zimple even in the street tiles. It doesn't seem fair since Zimpel was a surveyor and mapmaker! **See: Hennessy, Wisteria**

ZION CITY See: Gert Town

ZULU The Zulu Social Aid & Pleasure Club doubles as an African American Carnival krewe which parades on Mardi Gras. The gold and glittered coconut is Zulu's signature throw. Organized to ridicule the pretentiousness of other Carnival krewes; Zulu originally ruled with a banana stalk scepter and crown made from a can of lard. **See: Big Shot, Coconut Bill, Lundi Gras, Throw**

ZYDECO (ZAH dah ko) is an accordion-based, modern expression of African American and French Creole music originally from the prairies of south-central and southwest Louisiana. It is not Cajun in origin but blends elements of the blues and Cajun music with the addition of the vest frottoir or washboard. Zydeco is believed to somehow translate into snap bean. **See: Cajun, Creole**

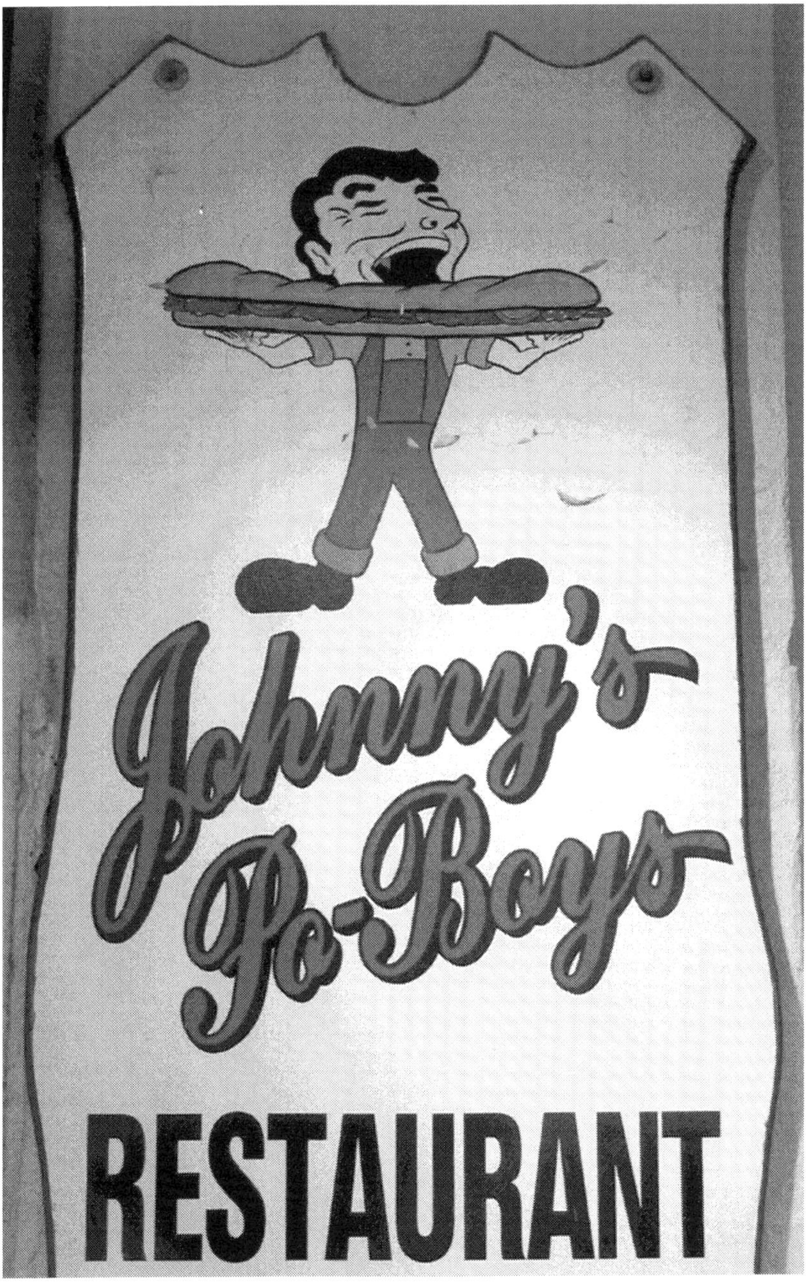
Johnny's
Po-Boys
RESTAURANT

ABOUT THE AUTHOR

Kevin J. Bozant was born in the Upper 9th Ward of New Orleans – as luck would have it – just a few blocks from Huerstel's Bar and Little Pete's Seafood Restaurant. He is a local author, photographer and digital graphic designer for his publishing company, Po-Boy Press – New Orleans.

His professional experience includes Warner Brothers, CW and ABC television affiliates. Kevin specialized in color print graphics for marketing and promotional materials as well as special events coordination. He eventually became senior graphic designer for the news, sports and weather departments. He was font operator for fifteen seasons of *Friday Night Football* as well as *Saints Sideline* with Ed Daniels. Kevin provided technical assistance on location shoots for *Real New Orleans* with Ronnie Virgets, *Crescent City Country* with Kim Carson. He co-produced *New Orleans after Midnight* with Bernie Cyrus and developed and co-produced *The Southern Garden* for Vitascope Television. He also served as studio graphics manager and question writer for Brandon Tartikoff's popular New Orleans trivia game show *N.O. It Alls*.

Kevin showcased his warped opinion of local politics and culture as writer and editor of the "Crescent City Crier" a political cartoon published by Gambit Weekly. He is author and editor of *Port & Burgundy 1840-1990:* A Pictorial History covering 150 years of St. Paul German Lutheran Church and Faubourg Marigny; *Quaint Essential New Orleans*: A Crescent City Lexicon; *African American New Orleans:* a Guide to 100 Civil Rights, Culture and Jazz Sites; *Crescent City Soldiers:* Military Monuments of New Orleans; *Music Street New Orleans:* A Guide to 200 Jazz, Rock and Rhythm & Blues Sites as well as *Crescent City Saints:* Religious Icons of New Orleans.

Kevin's favorite cultural experience was serving as personal assistant to Dr. Momus Alexander Morgus for his Halloween appearances at the Audubon Zoo. He currently resides in the Gentilly Terrace and Gardens Neighborhood of New Orleans.

poboypress@yahoo.com
www.amazon.com/author/kevinjbozant

Sample downloads available at:
www.independentauthornetwork.com/kevin-j-bozant.html

Made in the USA
Lexington, KY
24 April 2016